v v v

# Fractured Light

v v v

Copyright 2004. Poems are copyright the owners listed.

This book is a work of fiction. Names, characters, places, and incidents either are products of the author's imagination or are used fictitiously. Any resemblance to actual events or locals or persons, living or dead, is entirely coincidental.

All rights reserved, including the right of reproduction in whole or in part in any form.

# Foreword

In poetry, we try to "show don't tell" the fragments of our experience with the human condition. In this collection of poems, we'll show you the brokenness and resilience that shape our lives. The title "Fractured Light" embodies two aspects of our creations:

"Fractured" in the title speaks to the cracks in our armor, the wounds we carry, and the challenges we face. We are all in some way, broken.

"Light" is a huge part of photography, where you focus a camera on an object to capture it as a moment in time. In poetry, we also focus our lens on the world around us, but our medium is language. Through metaphor and imagery we illuminate the intangible, explaining through metaphor emotions and experiences that might otherwise be too cliché or difficult to explain.

This anthology contains a wide variety of poems, but primarily explores themes that confront the darkness of love, loss, hope, and despair.

May these poems inspire you, challenge you, and show you the flicker of light that's always waiting to be found.

# Table of Contents

| | |
|---|---|
| Carole Thewsey - Upside Down | 1 |
| Arlice W. Davenport - Answer Back | 2 |
| Kevin Meechan - Stains | 4 |
| Jessica C. Wheeler - Cycles | 6 |
| Heather Porterfield - Being | 7 |
| Roxana Eleonora Lupse - Kiki, the Frost Bird | 8 |
| Jeff Bachant - A Cat Has Died | 10 |
| Marta Green - Full Circle | 12 |
| Andrew Huang - Living Room View | 14 |
| Jacqueline Hird - Hills stretch into tomorrow | 16 |
| Rebecca Ebling - It's rare to see good days | 18 |
| Lexi Tasker - Summer Days | 20 |
| Jan Hayfield - Won't look back | 22 |
| Roberta Magers - I Will Miss Her | 24 |
| Cindy Barth - Learning to Walk | 26 |
| Monica Samantha Sanchez - Love's Price | 28 |
| Kathryn Kass - Fish Tale | 29 |
| Charles Bateman - The candidate | 30 |
| Susan Arena - Falling Leaves | 31 |
| Susannah Cooper - Ragdoll | 32 |
| Kelsey Burke - our dream is Yours | 33 |
| Charles Gradante - the doyenne | 34 |
| Ken Smith - The day the mirror sighed | 36 |
| James Warren - Rainfalls | 37 |
| Allix Dg - Spark // stoke the flames | 38 |
| Jenni Taylor - Sea of Rage | 39 |
| Lonna Lewis Blodgett - Ennui, Nothing to Say About It | 40 |
| Lincoln Blackwell - Summer Views | 42 |
| Kathryn Kass - Cord In A Minor Key | 43 |
| Jeffery Oldewurtel - Sushi Sue | 44 |
| Sean Cooke - Journey | 45 |
| Adam Casole-Buchanan - An Ode to Belgrade | 46 |

| | |
|---|---|
| Glenn Currier - Lightness of Doubt | 47 |
| Stanley J. Kaczmarek, Jr. - Castle To Castle | 48 |
| Lorri Ventura - Sanctuary | 49 |
| Tom Higgins - The Brisk Mountain Air | 50 |
| Debra Lalli - Dragonfly Prisms | 52 |
| Malcolm Wernestrom - wolf child | 54 |
| Lorri Ventura - Ode to Those in a Trauma Center Waiting Room | 56 |
| Charles Gradante - last night | 58 |
| Mihaela Stoian - Fractured Winds | 60 |
| Dorianne Retalic - Flawless | 62 |
| Alwyn Barddylbach - Flowers on the Moon | 63 |
| Kemi Roberts - Cigarette and Coffee | 64 |
| Elizabeth Mateer - Moon Child | 66 |
| Bobby Shannon - A Mountain to Stare | 68 |
| Sean E. Mallon - The Aura of a Rainbow | 70 |
| Theresa Sullivan - Blue on Black | 71 |
| Toma Adrian Robert - The Butterfly | 72 |
| John L Zwerenz - Dusk | 74 |
| Jesse Fenix - I'm losing myself | 75 |
| Courtney Weaver Jr. - The Vast Wilderness | 76 |
| Lonna Lewis Blodgett - Uplifted | 78 |
| Lockdown Larcs - A Passing Tree | 79 |
| Aimee Jones - Parts | 80 |
| Susan B. Cowdell - A Beautiful Spirit | 82 |
| Royce Earnest Rasmussen - Triumphant | 84 |
| Robert J Owens - The Fractured Lights | 86 |
| Chad Jones - Sins Of The Wolf | 88 |
| Sheila Blaxill - In joy I found my wings | 89 |
| Tara Karraway - Openrelations #Grownfokklure | 90 |
| Patricia Swan - A Poem of Love | 92 |
| Jason E Keeton - With what to build our temple | 94 |
| Brian Lee Rouley - Writing Funhouse Mirrors | 95 |
| Andy Altizer - She Gave Up On Me | 97 |
| Jim Beitman - a lesson from grief | 101 |
| Adelina Morris - And There He Was | 102 |

| | |
|---|---|
| Maxwell Sebastian Burchett - Someday | 104 |
| Patricia M Batteate - Secret Friends | 106 |
| Sindy Mitchell - The Long Path | 108 |
| James Lee Hardin - Lonely road | 110 |
| Heather Wegner - Aspiring Sun | 111 |
| Charles Gradante - isabella | 112 |
| Jenni Taylor - Mending a Broken Wing | 114 |
| Nancy Carol Warrender - Patterns of sunlight | 115 |
| Christina Hough - Here With You | 116 |
| Vinny Kreyer - Injected Fear | 118 |
| Ryan James Coy - The Storm Is Over | 120 |
| Theresa Sullivan - The Back Streets of Dunfermline Town | 125 |
| Simon M. Macy - Grant Your Wish | 126 |
| Maxwell Sebastian Burchett - Heartbreak | 128 |
| Patricia M Batteate - Wait Mom | 130 |
| Nicole Shunk - Patience | 132 |
| Andy Altizer - My Umbrella | 134 |
| Charles Gradante - unforgettable storm | 136 |
| Trevor Johnston - Deciphering a delusion | 138 |
| Jasmine Catherine Therese Bonner - Pain | 139 |
| Lorri Ventura - haiku | 140 |
| Carl Roussell - Untitled #11 | 141 |
| Marianna Crowl - Good | 142 |
| A P Cutler - If Only | 143 |
| Sharon Kingrey - Tenacity | 144 |
| Chad Jones - The Werewolf's Claim | 145 |
| Ervin Haye - beauty in imperfection | 147 |
| Tiffany Petty - Self-love | 149 |
| Phoenix Koff - They Ask me Why I Love the Night | 150 |
| The Inner Lens - Threads of False Piety | 152 |
| Monica Samantha Sanchez - Blue Mark | 153 |
| Josehf Lloyd Murchison - Melodious Verse | 154 |
| Angel Morgan - Remember Me | 155 |
| Charles Gradante - cowboy games | 156 |
| Kathryn Kass - What's In A Name? | 158 |

| | |
|---|---|
| Christina M. Cuevas - With God, You Can Overcome Anything | 161 |
| Maxwell Sebastian Burchett - No Stopping Now | 162 |
| Paul Crocker - Love Me Broken | 164 |
| ALIA Cook - The War Within | 165 |
| Jim Beitman - we have to let go | 166 |
| James Warren - Untitled 1 | 167 |
| Raul Alvarez Viramontes - Solitude | 168 |
| Sophia Kliatchko - Mosaic Heart | 169 |
| Charles Bateman - The cure | 170 |
| Jason E Keeton - An inquiry worth everything | 171 |
| Sam Y. Berry - A light in the dark | 172 |
| Nancy Carol Warrender - The Best December Ever | 174 |
| Robert J Owens - Each Dawn I Die | 176 |
| Elizabeth Brushia - God's Paintbrush | 177 |
| Adelina Morris - The Eyes | 179 |
| Nicole Shunk - Broken Path | 180 |
| Dr. Monica Discolo - I'm only here because of you | 182 |
| Marcus Taylor - Mother can you hear me.. | 183 |
| Gordon Hoffman - Barbara | 184 |
| Manju Kabba - Halt It Now | 186 |
| Gregory Bernal - Angel's Kiss | 188 |
| Laura Gallagher - I miss | 189 |
| Nancy Carol Warrender - Dragon Fruit Punch | 190 |
| Dr. Nafees Alam - Strong, Intelligent Man's Pledge | 192 |

[ Carole Thewsey ]
# Upside Down

The world looks so much better
When I'm hanging upside down
The people all stand on their heads
And smile instead of frown

The birds swim in the grass so blue
Dogs backstroke through green sky
And trees reach down with branches
That have sprung from trunks up high

The daisies and the buttercups
All smile and dance above
And under all the sun beams up
To fill the world with love.

_____

An English nurse who has always had a vivid imagination and loves the places it takes her to. Has written poetry since she was in school and who, although now retired, hopes one day to get it right. Allpoetry.com/Cassie_Hughes

[ Arlice W. Davenport ]

# Answer Back

I wake to a world
beyond all reckoning
I strip the birch
war strews
its bloody bundles
across the porous soil
failed crops
faded braids
of glory

my love looms
like a fortress
stuffed with endless
goods ammunition
gunpowder flint
I aim the rifle
cock the hammer
squeeze the trigger
a loud click
and nothing happens
nothing ever happens
except this planet turns
just the same and we on it
bow down to its delicate
balances its battlements
as thick as an elephant's gut

I once had time
to count the victories
notched in stone
now numbness wraps
its fingers around
my neck now I feel only
a jagged pulse
beat of a distant drum
a song of love
that encases
my heart with bear fat
and the grease
from an iron skillet
bang it against the birches
soon tall spirits
will answer back

---

I have been writing poetry for 53 years and am still learning. I'm also still striving for excellence. I have published four full-length books and two chapbooks. A fifth volume is on the way. Enjoy. Allpoetry.com/arliced

[ Kevin Meechan ]
# Stains

animals track scent,
mate in the open

will eat shoot and leaf
while sex starved souls
hide their fire
and give off nothing

me and the virgin mary,
stare at her face
words spill like water
from a lidless pot

fuck me and I bleed,
slurping froth
from her coffee cup
smack the bottom
of the ketchup bottle
to drain the last drop
anything real is used up
I toy with red meat,
building an ark

make a career fixating on ideas

one and one two,
x marks our spot

stuff of dreams a new sun,
you strike a match
and somewhere there's a god

fresh fields holding yesterday's heat

but you can't unpick a flower, take the wind out of her hair

use threadbare words to boot
shine my shoes
on her welcome mat, when coming home a quiet affair

beyond compare  roaring fires leave glowing coals, visions of sunset

hang around trees, brown burning bodies

while agog is sleeping like a logarithm,
us dying the square route
in uncrumpled sheets

white paper's immaculate conception.

———————

I am Scottish. Poetry helps keep the wolves from the door and the door open. I like walking with my kids and looking in the mirror
Allpoetry.com/Kevin_Meechan

[ Jessica C. Wheeler ]

# Cycles

A deep breath
of crisp October air
fills her little lungs
as day dips in the distance

leaves tremble, and they fall
from trees onto the path
she grows before my eyes
deciding she'll not follow

shedding extra wheels
she wobbles into balance
soaring on tires of two
across an autumn canvas

hours slip away with the sun
a watching moon appears
she rides across the stars
upon a brand new cycle

———————

Jessica C. Wheeler is a writer from Branford, CT, where she currently resides with her husband and two young daughters. Allpoetry.com/Jessica_C._Wheeler

[ Heather Porterfield ]
# Being

Nobody is anybody for very long
You learn the dance, they change the song
Plant a tree to flourish and bloom
Rest under its shade in the afternoon
The winter arrives with its cold and gray
Scatters the lovely respite away
Perhaps the best a fellow can say
Is, 'Who is it I must be today?'

---

A Health and Wellness Coach, writer, and vocalist from Texas.
Enjoy my family, dog, and gardening.
"Poetry- where I put my stuff." -Heather Allpoetry.com/H74soul

[ Roxana Eleonora Lupse ]
# Kiki, the Frost Bird

Crème brulée, vanilla-dripping
cream puffs, and jasmine tea
While heavy snowfalls come to bring
the jolly news of closed schools
on Monday, just before the clock strikes 7,

A polished A-frame bird house
With more than one entry
And round windows, plus a
popsicle stick porch, painted blue,
With dragon's blood sedum in a tiny eggshell

Look even more beautiful
As this bird house is covered by
A sparkling, snowflake-woven cap
And it has a frost bird next to it,
With wings of water that froze on a thuya

Stealing the branch's lace pattern,
A bird with a beak made of icicles
And pine buds for eyes.
It takes a frost bird, not a snowman
To carry snowflakes back into the lit-up clouds.

Fetti Poetti is from Baia Mare, Transylvania, Romania. She compares writing poetry with jewelery-making, and nature is her number one source of inspiration. Allpoetry.com/Fetti_Poetti

[ Jeff Bachant ]

# A Cat Has Died

Mr. Sumo, when you died we kept you
in a cake box, in the refrigerator, in the garage.
The pet crematorium was closed till Tuesday.

My daughter covered you with red salvia,
Bachelor's Button, yellow Henry Fonda rose.
Death was new to her, she needed to open the door,
peek at your lifelessness, poke at your stiffness.

Now, after months, I recall your quiet paws,
stuffed mice in corners, shabby sofas.
This house does to memories as evening light,
through a window, does to dust,
seen hanging in the air, settled on the floors,
paw prints, broken keepsakes on the mantle.

Your tail with a kink, congenital, folded back.
You slipping through doors, lost, hiding from love
and coyotes, reflexes faster than a rattlesnake.
I caught you-three times-in a live trap,
after nights of hissing opossums, baby skunks.
Feigning detachment at your return to the hearth,
your secret adventures, Mr. Sumo, prowling the fence lines.

I think of your standoffish cat nature.
After your death my wife brought home two kittens,

new born, abandoned, placentas attached.
Birth, death, squishy, liquid, the same ocean.
We bottle fed them, now they ambush the dog.
You'd pretend to ignore them, swish your bent tail.
My daughter's favorite is the little tuxedo, like you.

I'm getting tired of pets dying, Mr. Sumo. Just to say it.
Time's footsteps fall faster, turning the corner, down the hall.

The kittens are asleep, purring, I work my fingers
through the pads of their paws, pricked by little claws.
My daughter is sleeping. The house is quiet.
My mind drifts through its rooms, then onto some dark ocean.
Let us drift upon these currents a bit longer, my friend, you and I,
floating through dust, sounding the stillness.

---

I'm an academic in Southern California. I haven't been writing poetry very long. Started during the pandemic. Words have always come, just never wrote them down.
Allpoetry.com/Blue_Eyed_Grass

[ Marta Green ]

# Full Circle

spring is finally here
I open the windows, clean smelling air
silence in the early morning
dew covered grass like glittering rays of sun
yellow bumble bees hovering over creamy roses
playing until brilliant street lights come on
raucous laughter of children, heard over splashing

summer sneaks in
denim blue shorts and cotton t-shirts
bikinis cover women lying on chaise lounges
sunning like walruses on a San Diego Beach
sunrays feel so comfortable
wanting to stay in rays until skin feels burning
clear, bubble like blisters form on shoulders
air smells hot yet clean and radiantly fresh

autumn comes in gradually
cool winds whip long hair around
multi colored wind breakers cut the cool breezes
temperatures cause bright foliage cascading
like a water fall from tall, strong oak trees
banana yellow, carrot orange, chocolate brown
chilly air dries out leaves leaving them crunchy
raking and bagging, it is dinner time

steaming roast beef, silky potatoes, broccoli
desert, hot apple pie, a scoop of vanilla ice cream

winter blast in with air that irritates skin
making air burn nostrils and ears
five feet of snow float down like angelic stars
sitting inside, hearing the wind howl
sipping on hot chocolate
floating marshmallows, sweet dreams
covered in a red robe, matching fuzzy slippers
comfortable watching the magic come down
kids are warming clothing by steaming radiators
putting on winter clothes, down stairs they go
hot oatmeal with cinnamon, sugar and butter
eating, patiently waiting to go outside
making snow angels, snow men, licking ice cycles
it is a long last season, full circle will come soon

---

Marta Greens passions are writing poetry, short stories and soon a novel. She loves her family which includes three sons, two daughters and five grandchildren. Marta has rescued four indoor cats! Allpoetry.com/Marta_Green

[ Andrew Huang ]

# Living Room View

saturday morning—at 6:00 a.m—
does not shine that bright california
golden glow once framed the large
living room window to the hill.

ah po usually began
her morning routine early—before
there came barely a wink of the city
waking up to the dragging fog—
when she could play music loudly
from her portable cassette player.

she began her performance—slowly—
with steady arms, as red tassels
on her jian followed her movements.

she lunged forward—bent knees.
she spun around, readied to strike.
she gestured her hands backward.
she danced.

today, I nearly forget—snapping
out of a trance—how the sun
would peek in through the window
in brushes of bronze highlight
to watch ah po in awe.

the day goes on all the same;
it leaves only a trace impression of
a lost moment on the pane of glass.

―――――――――

Andrew Huang, a.k.a Change, is from San Francisco, California. In addition to poetry, he loves salsa dancing and design. Currently, he is studying Master of Architecture at University of Oregon. Allpoetry.com/Ah.Changeoo

[ Jacqueline Hird ]

# Hills stretch into tomorrow

As I walk the quiet path,
sunrise loudly replies.
Its golden brassiness
catches corners of my eye
as I wend my way over
the hard stone pass.
Chilled skin. Exposure
nibbles at the frozen fingers
poles, jabbing
the ground that resists
and crackles; snapping
icy sharp splinters.

A single " chut chut"
skims the dormant
skeletal heather, hiding grouse.
Munro you rise in tormenting
shadow etched; implied,
with orange crayon edging.
Weight falls on creaking ice
where watery worms dwell
then dance into hollows.
Hills wake to ginger scuffed
light stretching into tomorrow,
announcing I, as speck of dust

will one day fly
wildly into the squall.

As mountainside replied
"I am Highlands; welcome."

---

Jacqueline is from Perthshire in Scotland; she enjoys nature and what it can bring to her poetry. She enjoys wild swimming in the Lochs. This poem was inspired by a walk up Ben Lawers. Allpoetry.com/Jacqueline_H

[ Rebecca Ebling ]
# It's rare to see good days

My body is a mosaic of aches.

But today, for once,
it's not in the burning arches
of my calloused soles.
I carry my soreness in
tight cheeks, squinting eyes,
and cramps blooming
where giggles left my belly.

I've been fighting an
enduring itch, the one that
first prickled my upper spine
when the throbbing mass of bodies
glued their eyes to my fragile skin.
Its travelled down to my fingers,
so now they wave and dance,
scribbling to sooth the jitter of
the unborn art stored there.

There's a tight pressure still,
but today it moved from the
overcrowded shelf of my shoulders
to rest in the way
my sister's splayed hands

between my shoulder blades
pull me closer to her sternum.

It's a privileged suffering,
the pain I'm carrying today.

---

Rebecca is from California, and has been writing poetry since she was a child. She also enjoys painting and reading.
Allpoetry.com/Rebecca_E

[ Lexi Tasker ]

# Summer Days

Summer has clothed the earth
In a cloak from the rays of the sun!
And belts where the rivers run.
And a cloak, too,
of the skies' soft blue,

And now I swoon to the kiss,
The kiss of the wind,
And the touch of the air's soft hands,
With the rest from strife and the heat of life,
With the freedom of lakes and lands.

I envy the farmer's boy
Who sings as he follows the plow;
To the breezes that cool his brow
While the shining green of the young blades lean.

He sings to the dewy morn,
No thought of another's ear;
But the song he sings is a chant for kings
And the whole wide world to hear.

He sings of the joys of life,
Of the pleasures of work and rest,
From an overfull heart,

without aim or art;
'T is a song of the merriest.

O ye who toil in the town,
And ye who moil in the mart,
Hear the artless song, and your faith made strong
Shall renew your joy of heart.

Poor were the worth of the world
If never a song were heard,—
If the sting of grief had no relief,
And never a heart were stirred.

So, long as the streams run down,
And as long as the robins trill,
Let us taunt old Care with a merry air,
And sing in the face of ill.

---

I Lexi Tasker am a young writer. I was born in Maryland. I started writing when I was in 6th grade. We had a lesson on how to write and I instantly got attached. I never want to stop writing again.42
Allpoetry.com/Lexi806168

[ Jan Hayfield ]
# Won't look back

This summer,
after traveling a 1000 miles
she sits there
right in front of my eyes.

Two mighty rocks
grounded,
with serenity
looking at me.

I have my lunch
enjoy the view:
her beauty
in a sea of blue.

My hand is shaking as
I dare mounting hillocks
while cliff warnings say
don't fall off the rocks!

Then breezes flow
through endless fields of grass
fill my lungs with life
I let all stunning views pass.

The Skellig Islands
so close and yet too far
I won't look back
unless she, my star

sends a signal,
calls, shouts, waves
hoists a flag
I'd be back!

Just to see
if my water could
soften her rocks
break her shell.

But the Skellig Islands
stay at Kerry's coast.
Leaving Ireland now
I miss her the most.

---

Jan Hayfield is from Germany. He writes short stories and started to write poems in 2023. Poetry helps him to explore his feelings and to keep his mind off things. Allpoetry.com/NovemberMan

[ Roberta Magers ]
# I Will Miss Her

Dear Ann, this contest will forever be
within my loving heart
A special person who loved to care
and she showed us from the start.

Always ready to lend a helping hand
no matter what the subject was about.
She had a way of making your day,
as you smiled and wanted to shout.

I know your children will miss you and
others just as well, but life in you my friend
was so real, you never balked at problems,
but solved them and never walked away.

My last words to you my friend and it's
only here on earth, I pray to see you in heaven,
sip tea, and have a special time on our God's
special turf.
Thanks for being there when
I needed you, my friend. Your
love for people will never be
forgotten.

───────────────

Little Deer is from Corsicana, Texas. Right now, it looks like rain. This is a great time to write and read poetry. If any of you are like me, you're at a dead run when your feet hit the floor.

Allpoetry.com/LittleDeer

[ Cindy Barth ]

# Learning to Walk

As you step into the world
Without a screen, your hands unfurled
Eyes set free from gaudy glaring
So you can see and be more daring :

Step into a world of adventure
Embrace the beauty of Mother Nature
Look after her well by doing your part
Clean skies and seas, preserving Earth's heart

Step up to the challenge
Raise your voice against the carnage
Innocent children crying, dying
Proclaiming peace, your inner light shining

Step over the obstacles
Poverty, crime, pray for miracles
Help the helpless, hear their plea
Act with compassion, humility

Step in muddy waters
Prepare to serve in humble quarters
Make a difference, meet the need
Remember there are mouths to feed

Step out with courage, step out in faith
Do your part for the human race
Whatever your shoe size, big or small
Step out and leave your mark, love one and all

---

Cindy Barth is from Gqeberha (P.E.), South Africa, where she teaches music to high school students. Playing the piano, writing poetry and knitting are her favourite pastimes.
Allpoetry.com/Cindy_Barth

[ Monica Samantha Sanchez ]
# Love's Price

Missing the sensation
Of feeling
Depth of my chest beating brutally
Long to love again
& when I am placed
With the man god has graced
The man who doesn't bend
But he'll lock in place

I'll stay by his side
Safe space in his eyes
& Love him like

He & I
Have taken revenge
On this hard knock life

---

Aka FxNVxN/ Monka626 Expressing self while I dig up my heart, that I buried too deep.
Allpoetry.com/FxNVxN

[ Kathryn Kass ]
# Fish Tale

I browse in the basement of the old five and dime
while my roommate stands in line to pay the cashier.
At the end of one aisle a fish tank appears.
It is so peaceful to watch fish swimming behind glass,
mind stilled by water, the swaying of dwarf grass.
In this small, rippling world survival is clear.
The Angelfish chomps on the Guppy this time.
How startling to watch fish when death makes a pass.

---

My love of meditation, hypnosis, and shamanic journeying is reflected in my work and poetry. I live near the ocean in sunny, southern California, inspired each day by the beauty of nature.
Allpoetry.com/Kathryn_Kass

[ Charles Bateman ]

# The candidate

There on the corner   a presidential candidate   is passing out
animal balloons   in hopes of being lucky enough to be elected
to patch the air   leaking slowly   from a child's bicycle tire
his hair is wavy   the dandruff on his coats lapel   is equidistant
with his mouth   in dire need   of a listerine sponge bath
as now it stands   that anyone can be put into office   if they have
enough money   to buy votes from   senior citizens   in the lobby
of their retirement home
watching Lawrence Welk waiting for bingo to start.

---

I began writing memoirs and poems in my early twenties, I became a published writer two or more years ago. Allpoetry.com/the_budding_warrior

[ Susan Arena ]

# Falling Leaves

Dancing drops of liquid gold
as from an enchanted waterfall.
Twirling on the breeze like faeries
in golden gowns with copper clad wings,
suspended in a vibrant vermillion vacuum
until the wind nudges them
from their silent summer slumber.
Then, performing persimmon pirouettes
with the playful wind and tripping the boughs
in scarlet frisky flurries of tempting, tangelo tangos
they fall onto a crispy carpet
of cadmium beneath our tread,
shot through with spicy saffron silk.
Nature's palette of heavenly hues
is her swan song before winter's reaper calls.
with which the grey landscape is infused.

---

Teacher of English with a deep love of the arts in every form. A lover of Keats and Poe and so many others, enjoy reading and writing war poetry , romance and especially dark themes.
Allpoetry.com/Stellina

[ Susannah Cooper ]

# Ragdoll

Arms hanging limply, awkwardly standing, erect
Detached from the mainframe
Wide-eyed orbs fixated on a lonely cloud
Adrift in the expanse.
Lank yellowing locks suspended in messy plaits
Faded, frayed threadbare frock of scraps and segments
Fluttering around her knees
Swishing and swinging, threshing and thrashing
As she smooths down the insistent lumps
Of his glossy new suit.

---

Susannah Cooper lives in a small town in rural Kentucky. Poetry is the way she expresses her most tightly held thoughts, dreams, and fears. Allpoetry.com/SusannahCooper42

[ Kelsey Burke ]

# our dream is Yours

We think up a dream
and let the wind do the rest.
We trust her to carry it with care
to the birthplace of reality.

Luckily for us, she carried
ours right to you. Bundled
in your arms, cooing, giggling,
we knew it was safe.

Hand in novice hand,
you guided our dreams
down the eerie, weathered path,
hovering above every bump and crack.

Now it stands, fully grown spines
and limbs to stand on,
so we look up,
and thank you for paving our reality.

———————————

Kelsey Burke, from Montgomery, New York is an avid writer, and has been all her life. Writing is her escape, her happy place, and her catharsis all in one. Allpoetry.com/Kelsey-Burke13

[ Charles Gradante ]
# the doyenne

autumn has vanished
now the unbidden arctic blast blows

always the wind .. relentless
sweeps along the beach
swirls a vortex of sand
a wall of grain that blurs the line
between land and sky
too treacherous for walk

i remain indoors
crazed like a caged lion

the symphony of waves
through window panes
of sea salt mist
befriend me

when the storm inside me
gets too loud
i take a glass too many
to distract me

and

a doyenne
to soften me

Charles Gradante is from New York City, an engineer by education and poet by passion. In expressing humanity, the arts begin where words ends... whether it's music, painting or poetry. Allpoetry.com/Charles_Gradante

[ Ken Smith ]

# The day the mirror sighed

became the full moon
yawning, pale and alone
in its lonely room

peered out its window
at the impossible height
round as a nest

down to the river's silver
frozen surface
a reflected pool, it whispered

momento mori, 'remember
you must die – don't fear
to look the shadow in the eye'

the mirror's curved edge
gleaming like a crescent moon
sharpening its scythe

---

I have been an AP member for about 15 years. The immediacy of interaction with other serious amateur poets on the site is what primarily keeps me writing. Allpoetry.com/KenSmith

[ James Warren ]
# Rainfalls

As the water falls from the sky
each drop a tear from mothers eye
cities and towns so filled with smog
a choking hellish kind of fog

Her rivers flow across trash and litter
broken glass on rocks make it hard to slither
the oil that flows into creeks and streams
more often than not would muffle her screams

Lessons we've learned and soon forget
I'm quite surprised it hasn't killed us yet
if for our end we do not yearn
from our elder's mistakes we must learn

---

I am from North Alabama; I enjoy sharing my feelings through writing because sometimes It is hard to speak them. Allpoetry.com/Cosmic_crow

[ Allix Dg ]
# Spark // stoke the flames

Smoke may blind your eyes but

Given air
Given fuel
Given light

Warmth may fill your buttoned blouse

Coals may burn your fingertips

Embers smoking - smoulder bright

───────────────

Boxes is a heavy equipment mechanic from Vancouver, BC

His work currently focuses on challenging social commentary

He's planning a solo canoe expedition for the fall of you have any recipe ideas Allpoetry.com/Boxes

[ Jenni Taylor ]
# Sea of Rage

The giant oak tree casts its shade,
over the topographies of my being
producing shadows across gravel paths
as its branches spread spilling their secrets.

Streams create passageways to follow,
like tiny bronchi carrying air through my lungs
flooding within times when trouble,
sends turmoil diverting into winding roads.

A sea of rage roaring ahead of me
waiting to swallow me whole in its wake,
as I begin to enter strange worlds, struggling,
to uphold my sanity that's slipping away.

Waterfalls descending my thoughts afar,
leading my eyes to seek open vessels,
like a giant arrow pointing the way ahead
my dreams swallowed by the whistling wind.

---

Due to a car accident in 2002, I am paralyzed from the neck down and vent dependent. Most of my poems are about me, my accident, hope, gratitude, for contests and life in general. Allpoetry.com/Jtay

[ Lonna Lewis Blodgett ]

# Ennui, Nothing to Say About It

The ballast of our Thursday afternoon
in the countryside embeds in your smile
like day-old roadkill.
You yawn like a cow in the pasture eating sweet grass
hiding behind your words that flatten the moment.
Having no capacity of knowing
what you might see in an endless sky
you have redefined the emptiness of boredom.
Your small dreams have squandered the butterfly's wings
pathetically flapping 'us' into a prantic trance.
We lay like sleeping rabbits under an erroneous sun
that does not rise above the numbness
of your wintering heart.

Gridlocked like a dog's nose to the ground
on the scent of somewhere on a wall of many stains,
you hunt the missing birds sitting
on rainbows just out of reach,
then bait your hook to lure in the cold silver fish
reflected in diluted ponds of your resentment.

I wait…for a word never to be spoken while
you set your watch tightly
winding clock hands that spin in circles within your eyes
on a face of numbers that never leaves

its constant bemusement of wilted flowers.

---

Lonna Lewis Blodgett lives in Soquel, CA. in the redwood forests of the Santa Cruz Mountains. She loves to express in her poetry the beauty and nature through the gamut of the human experience. Allpoetry.com/Lonna_Lewis_Blodgett

[ Lincoln Blackwell ]

# Summer Views

Brilliant sunshine drenches my bones
Magnificently-stricken
Cooled only by the cotton clouds
A yelling squirrel
A distantly barking pack of hounds
Tropical breeze wisps through the blades
So lush, so green, so full of vibrancy
Jimmy Buffet and crushed grapefruit iced
Sand-buried ankles to my toes
A strengthening expressive gust
Thick pastes of cement gray saturate the firmament
Cloudbursts of fury, a green garden geyser
Canvas umbrellas soar through the yard
The sunny delight has died
Seven arduous minutes elapsed
Steam rises like spirits from the asphalt
Cotton clouds and yellow brilliance reign
Triumphant return
To the bespectacled milieu

---

Hello friend, I enjoy the opportunity in sharing some of my thoughts, poetry, and musings. Thanks for taking a peek. Allpoetry.com/Cyanidesun26

[ Kathryn Kass ]

# Cord In A Minor Key

Finger leaves gather sun
while darkness creeps round at the root.
Chainsaws buzz through bark
to the red cedar's center.
Death rattles the silent wood,
coughing up branches like blood.

Between broken boughs,
cut into stove lengths and carefully stacked,
small spaces invite the wind to enter.
Her warm breath seasons
the shaggy green slabs
pending blows of the axe.

Wood snapping,
fire flashing,
heat!
In the black of night, a tree of light.

---

My love of meditation, hypnosis, and shamanic journeying is reflected in my work and poetry. I live near the ocean in sunny, southern California, inspired each day by the beauty of nature. Allpoetry.com/Kathryn_Kass

[ Jeffery Oldewurtel ]

# Sushi Sue

Dust to ashes
Ashes to dust
Which one was hidden
from you all these days
hidden inside you
you lived in the air so shining
and the brother loving
And at times a butt in the
pain. Telling on you,
telling on me
No goodbyes yet
There are no goodbyes.
how can there be?
When you will always be
In my heart.
So for now sweet sister
I'll see you inside the heaven's
Morning.

_____

Such a hard journey
Pummeled from each side raining
Now lights through darkness
Vibrations good starting
as pieces pinched fall to the ground
Change....... Allpoetry.com/Jeffery_Oldewurtel

[ Sean Cooke ]

# Journey

The wind whispers to my left.
The moon illuminates my right.
I am grounded to the centre.
My journey's end is in sight.

―――――――――

I am a 34 year old man from northern England, reading and writing poetry is now a satisfying and productive part of my life. I thank my mother and father deeply and all those who read my poetry. Allpoetry.com/Arsenalfan30

[ Adam Casole-Buchanan ]

# An Ode to Belgrade

By the Belgrade streets, where two rivers meet,
The Danube and Sava bite ancient stones.
Where nights cast longer days, escaping heat,
The city beats of sultans, kings, and thrones.
Where unity's fire-steel forged Balkan lands,
Its fortress stands; a sentinel of time.
Sovereigns guarded many tales so grand,
Hard fought among many an empire's climb.
But, cobbled streets fill paths that we can roam
While mysteries still pass beneath my view.
I wish I could have known the Roman tome
That marked "White City" before Red and Blue.
I learned in Belgrade: history is made.
And I, a student, in its shadow's shade.

---

A sonneteer from Canada, Adam's work focuses on using the sonnet as an argument form. An amateur poet at best, he spends his days working in tech, his evenings drinking Scotch, and his nights writing. Allpoetry.com/Adam_Casole-Buchanan

[ Glenn Currier ]

# Lightness of Doubt

I feel it creeping up on the outer margins of me
like one cloud trying to overtake another
or dusk draping itself onto an old oak,
a dream trying to invade the probable.

Uncertainty seems like home to me
because when I think I have the truth
I find my way back home
where I can be the dismembered me
and grace seeps into the interstices of my mind
reflecting light in the puddles collecting there.

Doubt seems a dangerous companion
but I take its hand and pull it along with me
because it awakens me from my dusky comfort
and beckons me to the sparkling lagoon of inquiry.

Uncertainty is a favorite cousin
who on occasion texts me
with a pithy Punjab proverb
revealing a mystery worth chasing
to the dark side of the moon.

---

A retired educator in quest of his creative and spiritual side. He enjoys reading others' work and giving feedback that will encourage their creativity. Reading poems here helps him improve his work. Allpoetry.com/PoetGlenn

[ Stanley J. Kaczmarek, Jr. ]

# Castle To Castle

Castles...castles
Stones of paint
May it be
Tell-tale shadows
Of green-cutting leaves
Comes an evil night
Bearing an evil knight
A raging voice of his perilous sword
Stabbing, piercing the silence
Cutting my vision
Into blood-red thoughts
Raining upon the land
On which the castle finally rests
Harbinger of deaths
Assassin of breaths
Is it the wind
That brought the elusive castle
In which I might courageously live

―――――――――

I enjoyed reading letters that my grandfather received in childhood. I took literature classes in high school and college. I try to write poetry that a reader will hopefully find rewarding. Allpoetry.com/Stanleykaczmar

[ Lorri Ventura ]

# Sanctuary

The moon drops into the child's black-and-blue arms
Nestling there contentedly
As the little girl bobs across her backyard
Limps up the steps leading to her house
And ducks into her under-the-stairs bedroom
(A converted broom closet)
She gently tosses the orb into the air
Where it joins the stars she has collected
On previous nights
The closet suddenly transforms into a peaceful paradise
Deer graze in the gloaming
Fireflies kiss the child's nose before dancing away
A snowy owl perches on a tree branch
Serving as sentinel
The little girl scrambles into her bed
Satisfied that the world she has imagined
Will keep her safe from the dangers
That lurk in the chaotic reality
On the other side of the closet door
She falls asleep smiling

---

Lorri Ventura is a retired special education administrator living in Massachusetts. Her writing has been featured in a number of publications. She has won three Moon Prizes for her poetry. Allpoetry.com/Lorri_Ventura

[ Tom Higgins ]

# The Brisk Mountain Air

Time and place were arranged ahead
horses and wagon were the only way in
We parked the car in the Church yard
Down  at the end of the road
Uncle Wilson met us instead
taking us home in the brisk mountain air.

Prince and Lady, a mighty team
pulled the wagon and all of us
through the deep road ruts
on down to the farm
miles and miles and miles, it seemed
home in the brisk mountain air.

Across the branch not so deep
to the one-story house, where
warm summer days gave way
to cold mountain nights
sitting by the firefighting half sleep
at home in the brisk mountain air.

Oil lamps were our only light
besides the light of the flickering fire
warm feather ticks, fluffy down pillows
high poster beds with patch quilt covers

kept us warm through the long night
at home in the brisk mountain air.

---

Tom is from Galax, VA but now lives in Montclair, VA. Tom was a Carpenter, Truck driver, Preacher, Runner and Artist. He Loves the outdoors, and a simple way of life. He loves God. Allpoetry.com/digitalgrandpa

[ Debra Lalli ]

# Dragonfly Prisms

within distant veiled clouds,
misty raindrops pit-pat, pit-pat
rustling leaves like tambourines
as gilded rays wiggle through

microbursts of sunshine streak,
float and flicker in dragonfly prisms

A child runs and twirls across the meadow,
arms spread wide embracing the unseen,
an airplane taking flight fueled by the rush
of dreams swept on warm breezes

breath becomes deep and fulfilled

upon harps, angels strum the universal heartbeat
their comforting, delicate hymns are faintly heard
imagination takes flight into cottony clouds

wherein intuition searches for its mystic treasure

a child peeks from behind her mother's skirt
intrigue and fear play across the lass' face
wide-eyed, she learns from the dark
and from the light
that monsters really do hide under beds
while angels guard from above

the brook gurgles and drip, drops, drip-drops
little boys in rolled-up jeans and baseball caps
float handmade boats of twigs and leaves,
navigating life's many avenues
'til in deeper pools,
they find their course

against the trunk of the family tree
leans an old man,
his eyes a distant gaze,
locked in the heart of his youth

the song of his life pit-pats, pit-pats
and drip-drops, drip-drops to harps
that now pluck temporal
and sempiternal times

while...

microbursts of sunshine
streak, float, and flicker
dragonfly prisms across
the poppy-hued Elysian Fields

---

Retired from a livelihood dealing with numbers, but my passion lies in the arts. I enjoy all types of writing and love to draw. I'm a Tai Chi Sifu and hold a black belt in Filipino Martial Arts. Allpoetry.com/dml

[ Malcolm Wernestrom ]

## wolf-child

when she created her social media
the wolves circled around her
blank slate of a child
who craves adulthood too quickly
she saw they were wolves but only stepped closer
fell in infatuation with their scraggly fur and yellow teeth
they taught her their dirty animal dance
they gargled her and spat her out once her legs no longer moved
taught her to smile upon the reflection in the mirror
as long as they ran tongues along every curve
devouring her naked flesh
too-soon disrobed to serve slobbering predator will

her parents found her one night
with her ipad, without her pajamas
wolf-child couldn't see that they only wanted to keep her safe
the doctor prescribed self-love
and ordered no additional treatment
scribbled-upon blank slate emptied herself
when she had to report a man to the police
each identifying question a prod at her throat
convinced she had to disappear if she was to live apart from wolves
her body was institutionalized
caged in her own infatuation

years post-release, her brain still broken
pheromone receptors twisted and clogged
she adopted a dog
with filed-down teeth
broken bones from its previous owner
abuse rendering the puppy-wolf inoffensive
licking sweetly at her unvirginal flesh
as a child, she was the pet
now an adult, she became the master
half dead, still standing

---

Malcolm, a young Canadian writer from Tiohtià:ke/Montreal, was a 2024 FutureVerser with Poetry in Voice. Studying to become a social service worker, they enjoy writing in their free time. Allpoetry.com/malk-kun

[ Lorri Ventura ]
# Ode to Those in a Trauma Center Waiting Room

Together alone
While their loved ones undergo medical procedures
They stare blindly at a crookedly mounted TV
Offering soap operas at full-volume

They fan through dog-eared pages
Of months old People magazines
And gnaw on ragged fingertips
As their lips dance with anxious prayers

Around them, an intercom crackles
Calling color codes
That trigger storms of scrubs, lab coats
And rattling service carts
Flashing past

They pace back and forth
Across threadbare carpeting
In front of an aquarium
Filled with colorful tropical fish
Placed there to provide cheer and diversion
But ominously message-laden

With two rotund goldfish
Floating upside down at the water's surface

They pretend not to see the people
Who share the crowded room with them
Each one emotionally alone and unprepared

Like those in the throes of surgery
Those who wait
Hover between life and death

---

Lorri Ventura is a retired special education administrator living in Massachusetts. Her writing has been featured in a number of publications. She has won three Moon Prizes for her poetry. Allpoetry.com/Lorri_Ventura

[ Charles Gradante ]
# last night

with her... well into last night

the morning after
flashbacks flicker
frame by frame

slow motion consciousness

drifting stream of snap shots
intense intimacy of knots
images woven in twill
sensual touch at will

requited bodies of mulberry silk
slip into each other's desired ilk

ravenous wants
of panting breath breeze
the tongue of ecstasy taunts
while nascent nectar tease

nothing could stop
eyes of wonder gaze
for the scent of desire
and incessant kisses
that harbor moans of love's mire

her mouth of honey
that kissed burning embers
fanned the flame
that came

the morning after
the shadow of my eros
looked for her

i touched myself
to rekindle the glow

but it's not her touch

i lost my body
to her

last night

---

Charles Gradante is from New York City, an engineer by education and poet by passion. In expressing humanity, the arts begin where words ends... whether it's music, painting or poetry. Allpoetry.com/Charles_Gradante

[ Mihaela Stoian ]

# Fractured Winds

Thunder slipping through wrinkles of time,
darkness covers the blissful realm of rhyme,
howling through the stone forest, the wild wind
lays across the mist a mortal veil of rose tint.

Her story is written on an old scroll,
fractured left to fade in the sun
in yellow mist of autumn amber gold,
soaked up in silent moonlight
becomes a myth thousands of years old,

Her scars were born from the dark history,
glow at nightfall like a trail of fireflies,
soothing wounds left behind
by the oblivion of long-lost past ,
now asleep against the height of skies.

Fractured winds at sunset
flow through the dark void,
dive into the river of seconds
on a curtain of past remnants...

Moonlight floating through wrinkles of time,
darkness covers her silent realm of rhyme,
howling through the amber forest, the wild wind,
myriads of fallen leaves laid on eternal veil
of rose tint.....

---

I returned to poetry after 3 decades of silence.. In my younger years, poetry was a way of coping with my introversion. Now, it brings peace to my soul. Allpoetry.com/TwinkleStar

[ Dorianne Retalic ]

# Flawless

A dash of brightness, a sound of crush
Satin leaves fall softly, an echo hush.
Glitter in the morning light
Dance meekly in the wind it fights.
A sea of yellow sways to and fro
Liberated seasons a radiant glow
Stem stand unique as beauty unfolds
bright, withered dried, or dead
In every state, her charm is spread
Flawless is this sunflower bed

---

Dorianne Retalic, born in Klerksdorp, is a businesswoman and fitness enthusiast. After 20 years in credit, she launched Bubblegum Fashions in 2021. She's also a poet and aspiring coach. Allpoetry.com/Retalic

[ Alwyn Barddylbach ]

# Flowers on the Moon

Drunk love languishes over opal moon,
harsh words don't grow on trees, so better I
mark them up not wash them down with guilt
*and* if I still feel revenge someday soon,
transcribe it into song ~ banish my regret.

I shall not forget desire nor anguish,
words I later can't rely on, neither
shall I drown in bitterness and sorrow
as wars besieged by Trojan bribes and roses ~
those whiteout cratered moons and buried walls.

The common call at which our reason and
our ventures aim, the goal or chase, pleasures
tempered with unhappiness, too little or
too much, *sophrosyne* in Athena's bow;
the stars, Pandora's box, our progeny ~

Can man embrace them all?

———————

Aristotle argued temperance is a virtue, a person of sound mind will tend to do the right thing, at the right time, in the right way. But they need not shun all pleasures - AB Blue Mountains. Allpoetry.com/Barddylbach

[ Kemi Roberts ]

# Cigarette and Coffee

At dawn's first light you will find me
on the porch, with my cigarette
and coffee.

Reading the good news,
sin rooted deep,
trying to find the words
that will change me.

The wind blows a cold breeze,
that nip at my cheeks,
the birds in the sky,
swiftly flying free.

I take another drag of death on a stick,
if I don't quit now it will surely kill me.

The door opens,
my other half comes to join me,
his coffee in his cup and cigarette in hand,
I surely love this man.

The day must begin but I'll be back in the morning.

At dawn's first light you will find me
on the porch, with my cigarette
and coffee.

I was born and raised in Redding, California. Poetry has always held a special place in my heart and has gotten me through rough times. My father was my first inspiration.
Allpoetry.com/Allcriedout

[ Elizabeth Mateer ]

# Moon Child

Pretty,
make art
in pastel watercolors.
Decorate
your beautiful box
and dance for us.
Spinning, turning,
around and around,
on a drum of pins
going nowhere.
Never straying
from your enclosure
or the tune
of Moon River.

We close the box
when we're tired of your tune.
You can rest for a time, until
we're ready to play you again.
She was told
in less words.

She did, for a time, wait.
Followed every courtesy and restraint
imposed to keep her spinning. But

she failed at the task. Because she was wild,
a child of the moon.

And moon children
cannot stay plastic
in pastel boxes
waiting to be wound.

They need to be free and play
with kittens under the stars.

So she learned
that failure can be a freedom.

---

Elizabeth Mateer writes poetry and memoir about untangling how humans treat each other and carry those experiences with them. Allpoetry.com/Elizabeth_Mary

[ Bobby Shannon ]

# A Mountain to Stare

The river chills
and dances
from the newly mountain
melted snow,
the new rising rhythm
in its waters
has it
on the go

Filling its banks
with riches
to overflow,
rising to greet
the new spring green grass
nurturing it to grow

I stare in awe
and wonder
a gaping mouth
sight,
at the snow-capped mountain's
beauty
and height

The fluffy white clouds
near the mountain tops,

beautiful white clouds
without any
raindrops

The sun's rays piercing
through small holes
in the clouds,
where all but
near
the tops of the mountain
it enshrouds

I wish I were
a master painter
for this beautiful
sight,
to capture reflections
of real beauty
from the sun's
burning light

———————————

I like writing poetry in my spare time, I find it relaxing , sometimes challenging. I have worked at many different jobs in many different states. Allpoetry.com/Bobby6252

[ Sean E. Mallon ]
# The Aura of a Rainbow

I favor rainbows as they abduct my senses
The arch is a natural bridge and breaks down our fences
The technicolor rays shower over puddles
Leaving an imprint, nature seems infallible

The rainbow is fading and the sun has stepped in
Life continues, but a flawless image has already crept in

---

Hailing from Saint Augustine, Florida, Sean is a family man, sport enthusiast, and avid reader. Like other writers, he wishes to communicate through the most delicate of art forms. Allpoetry.com/Shamus_E._Malone

[ Theresa Sullivan ]

# Blue on Black

The mists climbs in through my windows pain
in all of her grey-ness she comes,
up, up from the blackened lake below
rising, rising she travels
carried along on the breeze of a moment in time
higher and higher she comes
these greying mists of time
these darkest memories
yes
the mists climb in through my windows pain

The mists climbs out through my window pane
until she reaches high above the dark blue hills
as far as the stars she travels
like a newborn foal she climbs
harnessing herself to our heart of Oneness
till she is Home with her mother the moon once more
yes,
till she is Home with her mother the moon once more
The mists climbed out through my window pane.

―――――――――

Born in Fife Scotland Sullivan is a poet whose work is rich in symbolism, weaving together her view of Celtic folklore and contemporary themes. Allpoetry.com/Theresa_S

[ Toma Adrian Robert ]

# The Butterfly

I am the butterfly.
I lie in wait for you underneath
thick pollen,
on the petals
of burning poppies
like your blood.

The wind picks up
fast clouds of dust
to high.
You come.

Naked you dive
in the tall grass. Wet.
Warm. You fall asleep.

I raise the wings straight
and before the jump,
I tense up.

Then I soar imperceptibly
furrowing the air
quick as an arrow
right under your closed eyes.

I send with my wings wide open
in wild rhythm
short flurries.

It invades your nostrils
biting
from your warm body
all the vigor.

Under the spell of the poppy
you dream.

I sip you
with brutality
all thoughts, memories, emotions.
I violently destroy them one by one
until your mind
becomes an empty blank space.

And I remain watching, for years,
over your puppet body and
the wide eyes stripped of all luster,
the only one left who can remember,
far from hatred and anger,
motionless under the sun,
relentless sentinel
of my devouring love.

_____

Poeanon is from Bucharest, Romania. Poetry is a spiritual path for him. 'Butterfly' is his debut poem published on paper. Allpoetry.com/Poeanon

[ John L Zwerenz ]

# Dusk

My dear Renee, I think of you!
Your kisses through the many years
Like a myriad of chandeliers
Has formed a stream of Sahara blue.

And in the evening, like two dark gems,
Your eyes take on a hue of wine.
They mingle with the rose and pine,
The charms which win all diadems.

The gleaming of your balcony
Reflects the vague and dusky tune
Which chimes of a wondrous honeymoon
When rapture blends with ecstasy.

Then all becomes still, all dins do die
As fountains sob in the square below
The gilded terrace next to your window
Where vespers rise and angels sigh.

---

John Lars Zwerenz is an American impressionistic poet and classical novelist. He was born in New York City in to a wealthy family. He has published twelve books of poetry.- The Associated Press  Allpoetry.com/John_L_Zwerenz

[ Jesse Fenix]
# I'm losing myself

My voice was taken away from me as a child,
and has not been heard from since

My ears are fishing nets
yet all they capture are insults and ridicule

I foolishly hid my emotions in a toy chest
now everyone plays with them

My blue eyes floated away
leaving behind a contrail of tears

My heart was sold at a tag sale
but soon returned
the buyer claimed it was broken

My brain was kept in a bottle
it drifted away on a sea of thoughts
washed ashore on the coast of a distant land
a little girl found it
she read my mind
then wept

———————————

Jesse Fenixis from Massachusetts and enjoys music, horror movies, zebra finches and writing poetry. Allpoetry.com/Just_Poppy

[ Courtney Weaver Jr. ]

# The Vast Wilderness

Surrounded by the embrace of untamed green,
The wilderness unfolds in living tapestries,
Cast with the golden glow of stray sunbeams
As they spill like dropped coins upon the floor
Of moss beneath, an earthy, emerald scene.

Within this open room the walls respire,
The thermostat turned rogue, a capricious sprite
That stokes a fever or stings with cold bite,
And we, clad woven shields or waving fans,
Bow to the whims of nature's fickle fire.

The larder's bare, unlike the stocked shelves home,
No sweets or treats abide in wood or stream.
Here, one must greet the river with hands keen,
Or cast hope's slender thread into the depths,
And wish the scaled and finned below to roam.

The rank and file of office sheds its skin,
For ancient orders set the chain of life
Where owl and elk might rank above man's strife.
We queue behind the fox with soft-stepped grace,
Our roles within the wild's belongings thinned.

Beneath the stars, the bed of needles spread,
Makes mock of plush and pillowed ease back home.

But hark, the night's confessional dome
Whispers secrets in the sentinel flames,
As autumn leaves their fiery ciphers shed.

It's there the doe steps light with curious eye,
In forest's chapel, we are but her peer.
We seek and forage in the realm of deer,
Parsing out nature's simple script of bark,
Where the branches speak in wind's soft sigh.

I tell you now, with boots bound tight for trials,
A daily dance with elements stern and spry;
The wilderness extends an open sky.
In the pull and push of limb and leaf,
Finds life its cadence in the measured miles.

After the roar of beast, the tempest's fury's spent,
With peace hard won beyond the scuffle's cost.
It is the vastness, not the coin, not lost,
That beckons with its breath of wild tranquility,
A call to be answered with soul's consent.

---

I just turned 67 and I have been writing Pier for a few years now and it makes my retirement worthwhile and gives me purpose. Allpoetry.com/Gray0328

[ Lonna Lewis Blodgett ]
# Uplifted

A vault of vibrant stars shivered
From the canvas of a dark silk night

Brush strokes of the blushing moon melts through clouds
In luminous inspiration as it slips into the sea
Draping across streams of silence

This calm, this resonate silver studded serenity,
This hush of contented skies,
This heart transfixed with fond identity,
A night of divinity, as beauty outwardly cries

I am born again
I am bliss with this realm's night
'forever' is mine

---

I am a lifelong poet and live on the central coast of California. I am a lover of nature and life and a spiritual explorer. I write to convey the quality of the human experience.
Allpoetry.com/Lonna_Lewis_Blodgett

[ Lockdown Larcs ]

# A Passing Tree

my love, our spring is at an end
who could trust the sapien
a nuclear red I see and feel
and to it, our being must kneel

mother earth, we did our best
to support life in your quest
but very soon, it will seem
all is just an impossible dream

so in the red darkness advance
no time is left for our leaves to dance
and yet in hope, time is the key
when sapien is done, in your longevity

oh mother earth, we trust in you
that we can sow seeds anew
once bane passed, we'll sense light
and join again, in your life's fight

―――――――――――

Lockdown Larcs, born 2020 to David Larcombe, in his 70th year, as rhyming insanity arrives with covid. An ordinary joe, sees a reason and rhymes just flow; an earth season or just something to know. Allpoetry.com/Lockdown_Larcs

[ Aimee Jones ]

# Parts

Can one of the parts of me that makes a person whole, find a voice, speak up, and tell the rest of me to stop,

stop being annoying,
stop being embarrassing,
stop thinking that it's me that needs to stop.

Can one of the parts of me be a little kinder to the others,
Can all of the parts of me learn to love each other,
Look each other in the face and tell each other they're proud.

Can that part of me that I can't change, and makes others hate me be accepted by my parts,
the others don't understand...

but remind the parts of me to be kind to them as they'll catch up.

Can one of the parts of me remind the others that they are fierce, brave and strong,....

never forget how hard these parts work to keep each other alive.

Can the parts of me that sometimes feel they'd be better off dead,
but still wake each other up to begin another day,
And never breathe a word about the time they felt happier playing dead;

Can all the parts of me forgive when they've been hurt,
love those who've hurt them,
and still be willing to love long after others would see something broken

Can one of the parts of me tell the other as long as there are parts,
we will never be alone.

---

Aimee Jones, to write a poem is the only way I can show the world what's inside. My soul screams to be heard through the written words. Allpoetry.com/Jonesaimee122_gmail

[ Susan B. Cowdell ]
# A Beautiful Spirit

In the sphere of love, where language falters,
a narrative unfurls of a toddler - three years young;
blessed with a soul swaying to its own rhythm,
Autism enfolds him, in a tender embrace.

Unable to speak, his voice is a silent stream,
yet his love is like a ray of sunshine;
It shines from his heart through his face,
illuminating the world, with pure delight!

His love is the language of deeds and gestures,
a pull; a tug; a motion that intertwines,
with the hearts of those he holds dear,
whispering ... I love you!

Intelligence is a flame that flickers in his eyes,
Conquering hurdles is a gleaming reward,
Though words may elude, his knowledge shines,
a wordless melody is written in his thoughts.

Independent and strong, yet gentle and kind,
he walks and runs, leaving worries behind.
With boundless joy, he dances through life,
A symphony of freedom, untouched by strife!

---

From the Philippines to the land of freedom,
I found my place;
With hopes and dreams and struggles to face;
I came to this land when I was young;
now, I stand with a life well-spun.
Allpoetry.com/Xuxa

[ Royce Earnest Rasmussen ]

# Triumphant

In the depths of my inner self, a labyrinth of silence unfolds, where whispers of the past linger like ghosts in the shadows. Each breath I take seems to stir a symphony of memories, faint echoes of perseverance and strength etched into the very fabric of my being.

I wander through the corridors of my mind, tracing the contours of invisible scars left by battles fought in the quiet recesses of my soul. Shadows dance on the walls, casting flickering images of resilience born not from outward strife, but from the depths of inner turmoil.

Within this hidden landscape, storms rage and subside, leaving behind traces of endurance woven into the tapestry of my existence. Each scar tells a story of survival, a testament to the flame that refuses to be extinguished, no matter how fierce the darkness may seem.

As I navigate the maze of memory, I discover hidden corners where echoes of pain and suffering intertwine with threads of hope and healing. Each twist and turn reveals a new chapter in the story of my resilience, an autobiography written in the language of perseverance.

The wounds I bear, both seen and unseen, merge into a portrait of strength, a survivor's silhouette painted against the canvas of life. I am the alchemist of my own pain, transforming suffering into power, turning adversity into an opportunity for growth.

In the dance between light and shadow, I emerge not unscathed, but triumphant. Like a phoenix rising from the ashes, I embrace the scars of my past as symbols of my strength, reminders that I am capable of overcoming even the darkest of nights.

---

Royce Earnest Rasmussen, an artist and poet hailing from Rockford, Illinois, USA, where he lives with his husband Aaron, draws his inspiration from the entwined beauty of art and verse. Allpoetry.com/REJ71

[ Robert J Owens ]
# The Fractured Lights

Spellbinding magnificent lights
Beam through the dark night
Blinding all of the occupants
That gaze up at the sight

Surrounded by the four elements
Earth, wind, fire, and water
Moses saw the same thing
Right before a biblical Slaughter

But life comes and goes
Like the beginning and end
And the fractured light is just a beacon
To where we're all going, and to where we've all been

Such things are formalities
That have been written in the stars
And if you read between the lines
You will see God's memoirs

He said that the earth shall be done
As it is in heaven
But only after the 7 signs of revelations
Have all come together

So embrace the fractured light
Because it comes with love
But you should also beware
Of the fury from above

So please, come as you are
Just like a thief in the night
For you are about to be judged
Beneath and underneath
the fracturing of lights.

---

krownroyal007 is from Los Angeles CA and has always had a love for poetry and song writing and would very much like to write a whole book of poems and create a beautiful and respected body of work . Allpoetry.com/Krownroyal007

[ Chad Jones ]
# Sins Of The Wolf

I am a wolf, but I am not Alpha.
I do what I want.
I am the Omega.
All life I will hunt,
For the capable beast.
To ensnare me, enslave me,
Keep me to feast.
His fee, his fi, his fo, and his fum,
Never enough to make me run.
His tempting with treats,
And his haunting vile smile,
Are what keep me here,
All of the while.
We laugh and we sin,
Day to day, over and again.
With Hell to pay, but not until then.
Only time will say how we end our day.
Seven deadly sins, seven days of play.

---

Chad H. Jones from Xaphanforge. I have been writing poetry and spoken word for a long time. Only in December of 2023, I started back up, due to going through a divorce. It's a wonderful outlet. Enjoy. Allpoetry.com/Xaphanforge

[ Sheila Blaxill ]

# In joy I found my wings

In joy I found my wings, a soaring flight,
A radiance that bathed my world in light.
Through a dance, my voice learned to sing,
And in the warmth of joy, I found my spring.

Memory too, has been my faithful guide,
In shadows deep, I learned to not hide.
From life that fell like rain on barren land,
I grew, transformed by a demanding hand.

Through joy, I learned to like every smile,
And in the depths of life's journey, we reweave.
For both are threads in life's intricate weave,
Teaching me to both take and to receive.

In joy, I found my strength and resilience.
Each one a step in life's race.
So, I walk this winding road,
Embracing all life has to offer.

---

Sheila Blaxill resides in Garden Valley, CA, in the heart of the sierras. For over 10 years Sheila has compiled several poetry writings, Sheila is a published Author through Amazon. Allpoetry.com/Seblaxill

[ Tara Karraway ]

# Openrelations #Grownfokklure

HOW They Admits YO Commitments OF Such AN Open Relationship AS IF Heterosexual AND Betorsexual Combinations
Mislead Samesex Persons Gayly BUT Oppositesex Ersons Couples Jyst Dont Sound Seemingly Right
TO Therightofway

Oppositesex Dating Bisex Outside OF gaysexUalitys
THE Feminine Nature OF Crossdressers IN These Arranged Rearranged TO Dateds OF AS Naturally Being Involved With AN Femmale OR Dominant Female AS NON Partners TO Opposite Sexualactivity Continuings Into These Couples LF Male&Female....Yikes
SO Really AND Various Ages Sleeping Around Dates AND Staying With Seperated AND Same Hones AND Around Where IN Headhonchos Withsrand Mistaken They ADS Really Claiming This Shit AS AN Open Relationship Parentingpartnersandmarrying Ouples This Pasts HP Bisexuala Tivity
!(Itsgeeatentertainingacceptingbut,  )


UM,

---

Video, photo, personal, self employed blogger. Spare time seeked fulltime opportunity for ads & spreadsheets for magazines. And selfexpressly on project working and about to get printed pubmy child. Allpoetry.com/Fixesed

[ Patricia Swan ]

# A Poem of Love

At dusk the corn husks withered and fell
The wind changed and brought a stinging memory
Of a once cherished love
I lifted a peach to my lips to calm my desire
When you are away I can see your smiling face
In every cloud. Even when they weep
They are your tears
Will you hold my hand when you touch your fingertips.
Then remember us at the lake
Together
Embracing a soft breeze and watching turtles sunning
On furrowed logs
The buzz of butterflies, lifting the fragrance of lily of the valley
to your flaxen hair
The rain will carry a song of the thrush
To where you are
Awash in the purity of the melody
Naked to the music of a shattered love
Do not cry, I am awake in your heart
As you are in mine
You will hear my song in your dreams
And know I am beside you

---

Patricia lives in Francestown N.H. She's taken up poetry along with years of watercolor painting. It has been a joy for me to combine the two expressions. They seem to go together nicely. Allpoetry.com/Patricia_Swan

[ Jason E Keeton ]

# With what to build our temple

With what to build our temple
it's like moonlight, a reflections debris
Tell me you're conflicted
and crumble what was falsely conceived

Orbiting the mayhem, precession
that delays the fading memories
Waste the commodity recklessly
and contemplate what not was believed

———————

Jason E Keeton is from Staten Island, NY. Following high school, he joined the United States Navy. While continuing to serve on active duty, he continues to chase his ambitions of becoming a writer. Allpoetry.com/Jason_E._Keeton

[ Brian Lee Rouley ]

# Writing Funhouse Mirrors

Beware the reflection,
It's unkind distortion.
Bending your soul by
Its careless contortion.

Might you have guessed, sir,
That fee for your entry,
Was your "En Garde!"
And the death of your sentry?

Your entrails displayed,
Spew your guts on this paper,
And that shield you once held,
Blown away like a vapor.

You have only yourself
Pray, rely on you only,
To thine own self be true
"YOU MAY NOT!" be lonely.

For this now you must do,
If you ever should dare,
See reality through,
A small burden to bear.

Your image, a monster?
Ah, ferocity's faith!
But a trick of the light,
Renders you a mere wraith.

How easily it ends,
As with all chosen strife,
Simply walk out the door,
AND GET ON WITH YOUR LIFE!

---

Write in rhyme? Who has the time? Then I read you, and I see who. So, thank you.
I have been labeled in many ways: husband 4X, father 1X, Stoic, Philosopher, Poet, and writer forever.
Allpoetry.com/BrianRouley84

[ Andy Altizer ]

# She Gave Up On Me

I did this to myself
But, my Self still hurts.
I entered this journey with nervousness and perturbation,
And left with absolute sadness and devastation.
I broke the rules, yes I broke the rules!
Without understanding that I had such weakness and was such a fool.
She Gave Up On Me.

Anxiety and hurting that few would believe
And then after some time and surprising change, left with decades of relief.
The journey has ended with nowhere to go.
Just when I thought there was a place no farther than below.
Progress made with appreciated knowledge and help
Only to mess up again and again to feel my heart melt.
She Gave Up On Me.

A Veteran with too much pride
Who only recently learned to confide.
It took a special person to get me to talk,
But too much talk would soon turn into an exiting walk.
Connecting with someone who seemed to care.
But now again, I leave with tremendous scare.
She Gave Up On Me.

I take walks into the wind,
Was, surprisingly, helping with this dark soul that needed to mend.
Ruminating replaced by meditating.
Pain and darkness seeing unknown rejuvenating.
Understanding perhaps in decades the feel for normal and unmasked
Just to feel devastated by mistakes that would again return beyond what the abnormal could grasp.
She Gave Up On Me.

Failing and flailing without fully knowing
Feeling, and really feeling, where I should have not been going.
Unable to grasp boundaries where I should not have gone,
Although such intentions would have been hard for me to fawn.
Willing to sell my soul for the hope of getting better,
Only to learn later that I was causing uneasiness, or even emotional fetter.
She Gave Up On Me.

Cries for help for second chances and to forgive,
Only met with silence designed to ignore and misgive.
Pain and suffering at a pre-session high,
With nowhere to go and no place to hide.
The mind spiraling beyond imagination
With only a clitter of hope, or really, just a silly fascination.
She Gave Up On Me.

Again, I must say that the mistakes were mine.
I had no idea on what to expect, or how wonderful I would find.

No appetite, no energy, no hope.
Working is hard, family is tough, and people notice my gainful mope.
Will I get better, will the pain eventually cease?
Will anyone help, or must I live in anguish and never in peace?
She Gave Up On Me.

My feelings for her may have waned.
But my caring for her will always be strong but surrounded by pain.
If only I could take things back and make my thoughts stay in place.
Then, I would still be learning and sliding forward with opportunities to chase.
Now with only thoughts of failure and being unloved,
I can only lie awake and seek help from above.
She Gave Up On Me.

Termination is never a word to inspire,
But even harder when there were hopes and desire.
Now, I wish I could say that time heals all,
I'm just not sure I'm capable of climbing yet another wall.
Tears are steady, and my heart still aches.
God I wish I could redeem my mistake.
She Gave Up On Me.

My lifespan in the later years were suddenly showing signs of mindfulness and surprise!
But now, the same ole worries and pain will remain until my eventual demise.

These words may seem corny and soppy, and perhaps even out of place
But you know that it's true if you saw the tears on my face
For I care for people who care of me so even then I know I must try
To get beyond the sadness burning my core that continues to cry.
She Gave Up On Me.

Termination to many is just another word for death.
It will be an unescapable placeholder that will follow me beyond the years and depth.
My semicolon will be with me until I go to my final home
One that finally grants me emotional peace and my demons from my emotional zone.
My humor was misunderstood, but at least I hope she knows that I'm full of sorrow.
And, It is my heart that bleeds for better times but, honestly, it won't be any future tomorrow.

I, Gave Up on Me.
;

---

Andy Altizer is a small town boy living in the city - Atlanta. He's always been a writer, and occasionally uses poetry as a means of journaling his emotions. Allpoetry.com/Andy_Altizer

[ Jim Beitman ]
# a lesson from grief

a lesson from grief
a broken heart won't kill you
it's humanizing

———————

I am an artist living in Noblesville Indiana. Writing is a great media that helps distill my feelings, thoughts, and experiences. It is always a great thrill to be included in an Allpoetry anthology! Allpoetry.com/Beitmanjim

[ Adelina Morris ]

# And There He Was

When I had given up on love, there he was
He wasn't just telling me words just because
He meant what he said and I felt this to be true
Believe me a man will change, if he really loves you
I didn't believe in this kind of love until I saw it in his eyes
And in time, feelings for him began to arise
Our start wasn't easy, there was pain
He wouldn't leave me, his love always the same
And when I'd get scared that he would disappear
He'd simply remind me, that he was still here
The hugs, the kisses and all of our laughter
You where what I was looking for, you were all I was after
And after so many years, by my side he still remains
And there he still was, showing me all men are not the same
I do, I think about, what if we didn't take our chance
Then we'd be missing out on years of romance
But, I also come to realize, I can't be thinking this way
And just had to learn to enjoy us, and take things day by day
In the beginning, there where so many reasons to give up just because
But, love had other plans, because there he was

I love you sweetheart... 🌷

---

My name is Adelina Morris. I am from California. I enjoy writing and I love that people can relate to what I write. I try to inspire and give to the paper 100% of my heart.
Allpoetry.com/nicoleray91

[ Maxwell Sebastian Burchett ]

# Someday

Someday, someday soon,
Someday, yeah, someday soon,
You will be with me.
I know that you will see.
Believe me when I say,
I will show you the way.
Someway we will find a way to be together.
We will never be alone,
It will be us forever.
When clouds roll in,
I will be your shelter.
Just hold on,
We will be together.

Sometime and it will be our day.
Stand with me and say,
We will do it our way.
Take my hand, and just hold on.
You and me,
Now and forever.

Someday soon,
Don't walk away.
Someday soon,
There will be a brighter day.

Just hold on,
Someday soon.

---

Max Burchett: a writer, singer and songwriter,
A crooner, a teller of tales,
A dream maker, soul shaker and captivator,
Hoping that in verse and prose he prevails.
Allpoetry.com/MaxBurchett

[ Patricia M Batteate ]
# Secret Friends

When a dog and a cat
Live under the same roof
There is never a dull moment
I have living proof

Always so nosy
One eye on each other
Like babysitting kids
Only I am their mother

Even while they sleep
Their presence is known
The cat loves his catnip
And the dog loves his bone

They put on an act
Just for human sake
They play their roles well
They are both in on the take

I think the dog gets jealous
Because the cat roams free
If one has an itch
The other catches fleas

They seem so human
It shows in their moods
They are even corrupt
They steal each other's food

They think they are slick
Sneaky and clever
I've come home early
While they napped together

It appears they are enemies
As far as that extends
But in secret they truly are
The very best of friends

---

Born and raised in the San Francisco Bay Area. I found a career as an engineer. A quote from Nightbird: 'You can't wait till life is easy to decide when to be happy'
Allpoetry.com/Patricia_Batteate

[ Sindy Mitchell ]

# The Long Path

Out of her mother's womb covered with an amniotic web,
An immaculate babe is born with a virtuous heart,
With soft pink skin that is soothing to touch,
Unbeknownst of the arduous journey ahead,
With long black flowing ponytails tied with blue ribbons,
Running blissfully in the green pastures,
Laughing in the glistening sunlight,
The rays gleaming on her sparkling smile.

As a flowering child,
Storms crackled in the midst of the night,
Shadowy creatures roamed in the dreadful dark,
And nightmares crept lingering in her innocent mind,
Her room twirled around with embittered voices,
Dispirited and desolate in her ways,
Vowing for a better life.

Having a mature face,
Travelling to the sandy beaches in ancient Levant,
She searches for love to renew her strength,
The twinkling stars embrace the night sky,
A luminous figure appears out of the shadows,
As she hears sweet melodies to her ears,
Having a mended heart,
They are one in spirit.

Growing old,
With silver hairs and a shortened body,
She has a heart full of wisdom,
She walks down the path with a cane in her hand,
Smiling at the serene heavens above,
The battles of the mind have been won,
And a red rose is left in the path,
With the wind blowing the petals into the air.

---

Sindy Mitchell enjoys teaching children and playing music. She graduated from the University of Toronto and has a master's degree. We are all a part of a journey in our lives.
Allpoetry.com/S._Mitchell

[ James Lee Hardin ]

# Lonely road

I walk this road alone,
with all the pain I've grown to know.
Day to day life becomes routine,
leaving you feeling like a machine.

Feelings of loneliness and depression,
wanting to feel ok, to not be a burden.
Work is a struggle from day to day,
forced to keep going, bills to pay.

You hope and pray for something to change,
though the idea of hope leaves you feeling strange.
Why must we always expect the worst,
feeling your life is somehow cursed.

You suffer through and continue to live,
trying every day to be constructive.
You go on, fake a smile or grin,
because you know the alternative is a sin.

———————————

I'm 35 and I've always used poetry to help cope with intense emotion or pain. I penned this poem to raise awareness that sometimes the strongest peoples, are in the most pain.
Allpoetry.com/LeeH

[ Heather Wegner ]

# Aspiring Sun

In young moments of lonely cold
how I yearned for another's hold.

I'd curl up & tuck myself into warmth
but my mother would abruptly retreat.
She'd say, "you're a black hole that steals my heat."

She radiated heat but was afraid
that I would take her hard-earned warmth away.
Oh how I wished that she'd just let me stay . . .

I am an aspiring Sun.
My motherhood has just begun.

---

Heather's a born & raised Alaskan. A wife, mama, nurse, & has only recently considered herself a writer. She's privately penned since childhood but is now ready to share her ideations with the world. Allpoetry.com/Heather_Wegner

[ Charles Gradante ]
# isabella

come to me like the wind
i will rain the flower
that gestures me

i will touch you with my thoughts
for love looks not with eyes
but with the mind

your kiss, your kiss
as brittle as a bluebell petal
our garden will assuredly bloom
everlasting wonder of bliss

silence of the undulous heaven yearns
as i slowly gather your languorous mouth
to shatter my will
dominate my desire

in your eyes
live a thousand lovers of my soul
the rarest love of all

love as precious as middlemist red
rarest flower on earth

---

Charles Gradante an engineer by education a poet and abstract painter by passion. In expressing the human condition, the arts begin where words end ... whether it's music, painting or poetry. Allpoetry.com/Charles_Gradante

[ Jenni Taylor ]
# Mending a Broken Wing

A past filled with grief from a car accident
a challenging time just after I turned 16,
not knowing what my future held,
sent me spiraling down on a path

I had difficulty pinpointing what I was seeing,
I got lost in the darkness of my fleeting mind,
entered a depression that was like being trapped in a web,
surrounded by pain, overwhelmed with life

After feeling like a bird with a broken wing,
I turned around, looking for the right direction,
searching for light to figure out which way,
I could break out fighting to overcome strife

Seeing my reflection in a cracked mirror
I emerged from within having self-worth,
In time, so I could finally fly again,
finding myself after nearly dying that night

---

Due to a car accident in 2002, I am paralyzed from the neck down and vent dependent. Most of my poems are about me, my accident, hope, gratitude, for contests and life in general. Allpoetry.com/Jtay

[ Nancy Carol Warrender ]

# Patterns of sunlight

Patterns of sunlight
in my room
on the floor, on the wall
warming beautiful naturally bright
continuing down the hall
swirling with leaves
swayed by the breeze
they do as they please
but I find it relaxes
it's April 20, I am done with my taxes
Yes I love a beautiful spring day
as the sun lowers in the sky
making its way
and I didn't say it makes me gay

———————

Born 1964 in Norwich, Connecticut. Bachelor of Science in Business Administration 1986. Currently resides in North Carolina. Allpoetry.com/Nancy_Carol_Warrender

[ Christina Hough ]

# Here With You

Pieces of me freefall to the floor in peace
They scatter like dying leaves from autumn trees
But after the dying is not the end
Like a phoenix the ashes will rise again

Memories are abundant and vast and true
Like space and time they'll come to you
They'll meet you where you are
And guide you like the northern star

My end is not the end
Because I will be born again
Through hopes and dreams
And found fond memories

My soul fills the ether, but can't be seen
But I am there and in the space between
You'll see me in the summer air
And feel me hold you in your despair

My body may be lost to decay
But my soul is here to live another day
So when you're feeling down and blue
Remember I am here with you

---

Christina is an independent legal professional from San Diego, California. She loves being creative -- often writing poems and lyrics, making jewelry, drawing, and engaging in other creative outlets. Allpoetry.com/MidnightGhosts

[ Vinny Kreyer ]

# Injected Fear

Small voice, no voice
vulnerable, I spoke up
and you
dismissed
me.
Feeling small,
trapped, lying there
exposed.
One breath, one
internal plea:
Do not
dissociate,
do not
abandon yourself now.

Then it was
over, you
moved on to the next
and I carry with me
the
voice
I reclaimed
The one you
Demeaned, anyway.

---

Vinny is from California where she finds peace and healing in the ocean and through writing poetry, where she feels heard and has a voice. Allpoetry.com/VinnyK

[ Ryan James Coy ]

# The Storm Is Over

In the dark the silence is so loud it's like a thunderstorm that never ends.

The tears that pour from my face is like the rain that is pouring down hitting the window ,and flooding everything around it.

Heart is shattered like the windows that broke during a tornado.

My emotions spiral like the tornado that broke the windows during the storm.

Then one day the sun comes out, the sky is clear; and the rainbow I've been waiting for shows its bright colors in the clear sky.

The birds are chirping the wind is light and the sun fills my soul with delight.

The  healing begins as the sun hits my skin; I feel the warmth of happiness once again.

Knowing all is right and all is bright.

The love and joy I find from not just myself but those  all around me.

Love from family is like butterflies on a warm spring day they're near and far.

Beautiful yet delicate. Butterflies show the way the way to freedom and joy.

The joy of being around the ones you love. Even the memories from those above is what helps guide, you through the storm that eventually will end.

Family is like the rain it helps you grow like the roses and tulips that bloomed that spring morning.

Like the spring flowers you also grow beautifully.

When you're around those you love you can also grow like spring flowers.

Sitting on the porch while listening to the chirping of the birds .

Watching as they fly from near to far ,and above knowing the journey just begun.

The love I have  is deeper than all bodies of water on earth combined.

There's no way to measure the joy I feel, when I'm around those I love unconditionally.

While sitting on the porch listening to the birds chirp.

Feeling the warm spring weather.

I sit there thinking………. what's freedom if we're stuck in the past?

Are you truly free if you're stuck living in the past and not the present?

Well……….. are we?

Sitting there pondering while drinking coffee staring at the sunrise.

The sunrise that's so beautiful it looks like a painting.
A painting of paradise, like you'd see in an art museums in a big city somewhere.

Then I start to wonder are you really healed if you're poisoned?

Poisoned from what you may wonder.?

Well the poison I'm talking about is poison from dwelling on past pain.

When you live with past pain it's like poison to the body and mind.

This is what slowly kills a person, making them so depressed, and miserable.

They can't seem to remember or recognize happiness.

Happiness may be recognized from the view of other people's happinesses ;but until you move on, your happiness isn't a reality.

Healing from past pain ,and past trauma is like when you're sick.

You're given medication to feel better.

The medication for this is simple forgiveness and love.

When there's forgiveness there's healing.

Then once you forgive it's like someone took off a ton of bricks from your chest.

The weight lifted from you makes you feel like you're sitting by a peaceful river.

At that point you now have freedom.

Peace in the heart and mind and enlightenment in the soul is the beginning of rebirth.

Rebirth is a reset button that erases all pain and trauma and allows you to have a fresh beginning.

The peace you get from living in the present after finding your own joy, is freeing like a baby bird flying for the first time.

Freeing like a loose ballon.

The joy you receive is like a mother seeing her baby for the first time.

The joy you have is like the joy you get as a child when you first go to Disneyland.

Life is an adventure it's beautiful like sunsets and sunrises.

Life can also be sloppy like mud, after a good rain storm.

Like walking in wet, and sticky mud after a down pour, we also can get through it.

Sitting here petting my beautiful cat and beautiful dog, breathing in that fresh Oklahoma air; I can smile with calmness in my heart and mind.

Knowing the best is yet to come and I'm finally free from everything that made me feel less than happy.

In time I'll grow old and will be able to join those beautiful butterflies I see fluttering around the big , blue skies.

I'll become the path for whom ever comes after me to walk on while I guide them through their journey.

When one tree falls after years of being strong , another tree grows becoming even stronger than the last.

---

I'm gay, 27 from Layton, Utah  I make poems as therapy for myself and hopefully for whoever reads them.   My favorite poets are Oscar Wilde and Edgar Allan Poe. Allpoetry.com/Rjc96

[ Theresa Sullivan ]

# The Back Streets of Dunfermline Town

Dunfermline is lonely without me
and the sea here has drawn so far back from the shore,
for my mind takes me home  to the backstreets
and I need to go back  there once more
for Dunfermline is lonely without me
and the rabbits they still sit by the door.

I am in love with that over-lay crowded  place
for it reminds me of bedtime stories for which I still long
and the sounds in the glen they haunt me still
as the robins song it holds  my heart so tenderly
and  a part of me still dwells and walks
through the memory drenched  Halls of Carnagie
filling my heart with longing ,poems and songs

Yes
Dunfermline is lonely without me
and the sea here has drawn so far  back from the shore
for my heart takes me home to the backstreets
where Holly and Reubus still sit by the door.
For Dunfermline is lonely without me
and someday, I will  return there once more.

---

Born in Fife, Scotland, Sullivan is a poet whose work is rich in symbolism, weaving together her view of Celtic folklore and contemporary themes. Allpoetry.com/Theresa_S

[ Simon M. Macy ]

# Grant Your Wish

Danny

The bottle flies passed my head,
hitting the wall behind me, glass scrapes away bits of flesh from
the blowback like a shrapnel grenade.
Her hands are unforgiving, relentlessly clawing and ripping at me,
trying to dig out her past mistakes.
The slurred sentences that leave her lips, the smell of alcohol
radiating from her breath, enters my nostrils making me want to
hurl.
After an hour she passes out in her bedroom, glass shards still
litter my messy hair and ruffled up clothing, nothing I'm not used
to.
I clean myself up and head to my room, but I don't sleep, instead
I look at my belt, sturdy leather built to hold heavy objects.
Everyone has a breaking point. I guess I finally hit mine.
I'm not doing this for her, I'm doing this for myself, to get away
from her, to grant my own wish.

Jessica

His team lost, and of course I was to blame for it, because
somehow me trying to get my homework done caused his team to
lose.
I don't try to keep my hair nice, it gets messed up anyways.
Makeup can make someone look pretty, keep the real us from

showing to our friends.
He compliments me then but spits on me now.
I don't cry when he yells at me, and I know how to position myself so the bruising doesn't hurt as much.
My dad is a nice guy, except when he drinks.
But tonight that won't matter anymore, nor will homework, or makeup, or messy hair.
None of it will matter. I got accepted into my dream school.
I'll get away from him, and finally live my life.
I'll grant my wish all by myself.

———————

Expression is art, and your soul is the artist.
Those are have suffered but still carry on, still go to work, still have families and still have faith are the strongest among us.
Allpoetry.com/SMM_Poems

[ Maxwell Sebastian Burchett ]

# Heartbreak

It was just last night, I dreamed,
And I saw you, yeah, me and you.
Then I woke up, and I remembered,
Yeah, I remembered you.
That time we walked down Fifth Avenue,
Holding hands and kissing in the snow,
Said you loved me at Valentinos,
Talking about love things.

When I recall, back then,
I can't even think, I just weep.
Just have this deep,
Heartache, heartbreak,
My heart breaks for you now.
Wish you were here, with me,
It's just how love has to be.
Yeah, I just want you back.
Don't know why love had to leave.
My heart just breaks.

When I first met you,
Thought it would be, I thought I knew,
A lifelong love for us two,
Thought it was meant to be.
But now I want you, I want you back.
I want to escape this heartbreak.

Wish you were here still with me.
Let's make our dreams reality.

Can someone tell me,
What can I do,
To fix this heartbreak.
Tell me true,
Do you still think of me? I always think of you.
Did your heart break, too?
Mmmh

———————————

Max Burchett: a writer, singer and songwriter,
A crooner, a teller of tales,
A dream maker, soul shaker and captivator,
Hoping that in verse and prose he prevails.
Allpoetry.com/MaxBurchett

[ Patricia M Batteate ]

# Wait Mom

Wait, mom, please don't go
I didn't say goodbye
Was your heart, so painfully broken
That you had to go and die

We never saw it coming
It came on so quick
Rushing you to the hospital
You turned so critically sick

I saw your eyes, for the last time
As they wheeled you to the E.R.
There wasn't much that they could do
The toxins had spread so far

I held your hand all through the night
I know, you knew, I was there
The presence of angels was all about
To answer, all of our prayers

Your tiny ailing body
Looked even smaller, as you slept
The private person that you are
Feelings, to yourself, you had kept

I was told so many times
To keep in touch with you, mom

But time unforgivably slips away
Here today, by tomorrow, it's gone

I wish we could have been closer
But not everyone is the same
I've made some mistakes, down the line
But never meant, to cause you pain

I just wanted your approval
Even if, my ideas were strange
I like to think, outside the box
As life, is the essence of change

So wait mom, just one more kiss
And one final embrace
Once you are gone, there's no going back
The moment, cannot be replaced

As I watched you take your last breath
I'm reminded, of how blessed I am
In the wake, of your departure
I can say, I now understand

All of the times, we had disagreed
For one reason, or another
Only to find, my mom was like me
And I, just like my mother

---

Born and raised in the San Francisco Bay Area. I found a career as an engineer. A quote from Nightbird: 'You can't wait till life is easy to decide when to be happy'
Allpoetry.com/Patricia_Batteate

[ Nicole Shunk ]

# Patience

I fear causing you pain
By changing our unspoken routine
Silence over dinner
Window staring in the car
Not holding your calloused working hands
I love you spoken in a whisper
I'm overburdened
With my broken past
That is unraveling our bond
Your annoyed I'm retracing my old steps
Leaving us behind
Serenity is something I haven't provided
Our loving connection unravels
I'm sorry while my heart heals
It's a transition
A journey I should of completed years ago
A heart that never had closure
Time doesn't heal all
I despise causing you pain
Your love is a beacon of hope and light
Your smile carries silent strength
Your laughter breaks old chains
You entrusted me with your heart
Now your skeptical of mine
A burden I carry

I dread hurting your heart
With my broken past
Patience is a virtue
Please find the strength
To hold me tight
While my vulnerability scares you
Our love story is worth holding onto
Even with my healing
From a broken past
Our love is worth patience and grace

---

Nicole Shunk is a southern born who call the north home. Poetry is an art that saved my life. Now I share my writing and hope these words help and inspire others. Allpoetry.com/Shunket23

[ Andy Altizer ]

# My Umbrella

I have not had a good umbrella for long.
I am not sure that I ever had one.
But, after having an umbrella, living without one would take someone very strong.
Having one makes the bad days, well, almost fun.

Storms are rough for people like me,
Keeping dry can be hard, especially when the rains come from the eyes.
Often hard to tell by others, but then again, it's the inside what they can't see.
That's when having an umbrella keeps away the cries.

Now, having an umbrella up is not always a need,
But when the darkness comes, it pays to have it near.
It is then when the heart will start to bleed.
And it is then when the umbrella will protect us from fear.

I wish I didn't have to have one to make me be.
I should know how to do without such a shield.
But, without my umbrella, I will surely take the easy route and flee.
You see, I have demons and worries with nothing else to help me heal.

I lost my umbrella the other day.
It came rather unexpectedly, and since that time the storms have been severe.
Without my umbrella, hopes and aspirations have lost their way,
Which can only mean that sunny days will not soon appear.

I Miss My Umbrella.

---

Andy Altizer is a small town boy living in the city - Atlanta. He's always been a writer, and occasionally uses poetry as a means of journaling his emotions. Allpoetry.com/Andy_Altizer

[ Charles Gradante ]
# unforgettable storm

walking the beach
my mind wanders
without focus
when storm clouds
appear

i approach
a seashell
it looks familiar

but that's me
always thinking
of you

to my ear
the shell echos
oncoming rumblings
deep resonant sounds
of a storm dragon

the shell carries
a memory

you ... me
that day
walking

listening as your laughter is consumed
by the sound of crashing waves
skipping pebbles
on the ocean's surface

only us
and the oncoming storm

just moments away
watching us
daring us
to defy its doom

and make love anyway

we looked at each other
wondered
is there time

your eyes .. your smile
unforgettable storm

———————————

Charles Gradante is from New York City, an engineer by education and poet by passion. In expressing humanity, the arts begin where words ends... whether it's music, painting or poetry. Allpoetry.com/Charles_Gradante

[ Trevor Johnston ]

# Deciphering a delusion

Drifting, seeming, I can see the next step,
Looking at myself, I can tell,
I'm spiraling outward and onward from a mentality, that shows me, that I'm losing my grip on reality,
And I'll say it's my life (to myself)
But I cant control it (my life is hell)
And I'll live within my lines (cautiously)
Towards insanity,
Gauging my existence, off of the, mirror that was placed on my wall,
This last bit has been tough
Love lost it's way, after all,
When you said to me, "you're going to be okay now"
But we all know, I've lost, my way down, madness, ensued me, but it's still not the end.
Maybe some day, we'll meet again,
You left me with, "you'll be out of this any day now."
So then, please, won't you tell me, when?
Because It doesn't seem to end.

––––––––––––––––––

I am a depressed person that lives alone in isolation. I tend to spiral into self destructive patterns. Therefore I write stuff.
Allpoetry.com/Trevor_Johnston

[ Jasmine Catherine Therese Bonner ]

# Pain

what is this feeling
that I feel in the depths
of my soul...... numb to everything....
I thought the nightmare
would end once sleep was upon me
Sleep and the shadows are my enemies
91 disturbances in a single night
that's enough to make a person go insane
It's not enough to be insane
How to explain the bruises,
That cover me
the missed day of work.
The sadness
the sickness inside
this madness comes from
the depths of the soul
like Frankenstein
a monster unwanted
unloved
unforgiven
forsaken empty soul

---

Ekaterina is a passionate reader and poet who has been honing her craft for the past three years online. Despite taking a break to serve in the military. She is now eager to dive back into writing. Allpoetry.com/EKaterina89

[ Lorri Ventura ]
# haiku

In order to read
I need a cat on my lap
Rhythmically purring

---

Lorri Ventura is a retired special education administrator living in Massachusetts. Her writing has been featured in a number of publications. She has won three Moon Prizes for her poetry. Allpoetry.com/Lorri_Ventura

[ Carl Roussell ]
# Untitled #11

A good heart is not as common as some believe

'And what can a good heart do?', you wonder
Transform her into someone beautiful

Her smile will light the dimmest days
Pulling him back from his self-imposed exile
And her good heart wonders, "Is this who I am to you?'

_____

Carl Roussell live in Hamilton, Ontario. He describes the , real or imagined moments and feelings in life. Allpoetry.com/Carl_R

[ Marianna Crowl ]

# Good

Everything is good
So very good
I will endure any bad if it meant the outcome of it all was good
There is more good than bad in this world
It is easy to get caught up in the bad
So easily that we miss out on all the good
Very badly I want to add good to the world
Doing so I can eliminate bad habits in myself
Good energy is infectious and others will desire it too
The world needs me at my best so I can radiate positivity
I must keep myself away from bad temptations
No longer do I have the time to waste on negative things
All good things meant for me will come
There is so much joy knowing the good days are never over in the midst of it all
I will be a good presence in this lifetime for myself and for the world around me
I will be the light in this world, and I will receive all the good life has to offer me
The best is yet to come

_____

I aspire to write more poetry in 2024. For me, there is a desire to challenge myself to write a poetry book in my lifetime. Allpoetry.com/MariannaC

[ A P Cutler ]

# If Only

A few words but just a pie in the sky really
Before I leave this world behind as I reach my final hour, all the things that I would change if I only had the power,
The sun would shine forever and no one feeling cold, all people would be young at heart and never growing old,
All poor souls sleeping roughly every one would have a bed, while all the hungry children would be comforted and fed,
Every soul who's drawn and worried with a tear drop in there eye, a warm hand to touch and comfort and wipe the teardrop dry,
No child would be an orphan, the mental sufferers would be free, no one born lame and crippled and all the blind would see,
Every one would have a guardian angel no who they are, then all would cross a rainbow to find their lucky star,
All the weary wanderers would no more need to roam, for the worlds lost souls every one would find a home,
Of all the things that I would do as long as I remain, I'd set free every aching heart and take away the pain,
With this power I'd travel round the world and as I go along I'd sprinkle magic stardust to put right every wrong,
Then everyone would have a friend with no one lost and lonely, If I had the power to change it all, if only, aah, if only

_____

A P Cutler is from Gosport and I write poetry as I have so many life experiences that I want to share with people.
Allpoetry.com/A_P_Cutler

[ Sharon Kingrey ]

# Tenacity

The strength of a flowing stream
is not in its fluidity but in
the pull of gravity, as opposition
turns the key to tenacity,
for the power of water lies
in its versatility - to be placid pool
or dread tsunami.

In life, it can be our noblest metaphor,
whether falling or flowing, fore there is
dignity in it's power to transcend
forces of nature, never deterred
by murky depths, as it is adept at
flowing around barriers, breaking
through restraints.

When crystallizing
it never surrenders or dies,
for water, like life is abundance
chafing against resistance,
occasionally even defying natural law
as it flows curiously uphill.

---

Gotlilt lives in Utah and is originally from Arkansas. Her passion is poetry, having been intrigued by words since early childhood. Member of Allpoetry for 14 yrs.   Allpoetry.com/GotLilt

[ Chad Jones ]

# The Werewolf's Claim

When I bark you shall hear me.
When I bite you shall feel me.
When you bleed you shall know,
you reached your limits with me.

As I bark you will be knowing.
That you are just a stone's throw from sowing.
Those deeds you chose to keep growing.
Until the festering became overflowing.

Doom it speaks as I bark.
Within the darkness no chance of a spark.
Once you hear a hesitation amidst the silence…
I am about to make my mark.

The mark a bite, a bite so right.
A werewolf incisors, clamped on tight.
You risk sudden movement with all your might.
Trying to escape but you lost sight.

This hellish form, a beast so clever
Brutality so fierce, a force of forever
The lurker beyond, arteries to be severed
All victims now known as the remembered.

---

Chad H. Jones aka Xaphanforge. I have been writing poetry and spoken word for a long time. Only in December of 2023, I started back up, due to going through a divorce. It's a wonderful outlet. Enjoy. Allpoetry.com/Xaphanforge

[ Ervin Haye ]

# beauty in imperfection

In the fractured light's delicate dance,
Resilience and brokenness meet, a perfect chance
To witness beauty in scattered pieces,
A story etched in cracks and creases.

Resilience rises, a strength unfurled
From pain's depths, it's never hurled.
Scars and wounds, reminders of the fight,
Each step forward brings a glimmer of light.

Brokenness, a state of being,
Yet in its midst, there's something freeing.
In the cracks, there's space to grow,
In brokenness, there's a unique glow.

Our pieces, scattered, frayed, and worn,
Yet in imperfection, beauty's born.
A mosaic of colors, a living art,
Each fragment a story, a beating heart.

Every fracture holds a tale,
A journey of triumph, never frail.
Though pain may leave us battered, sore,
Healing brings something more.

Resilience and brokenness, paradoxical blend,
Through the cracks, new hope we send.
Strength born from adversity's embrace,
Beauty forged in vulnerability's grace.

Let light filter through each crack,
In our brokenness, no turning back.
We rise stronger, each piece finds place,
A masterpiece of resilience and grace.

---

Writing poetry helps me think I like to convey my details to make the reader feel like they are apart of the story.
Allpoetry.com/Ehaye20

[ Tiffany Petty ]

# Self-love

Before we can love others, we must start
Within,
Embrace our own journey, let self-love
begin.
Nurture our souls, let kindness overflow
for when we love ourselves, our love will
Surely grow.

Take time for self-care, let your spirit soar,
Discover your worth, and love at your core.
Only then can you give love that's true,
When you've learned to love yourself, the
Way you deserve to.

So remember, my friend, before you extend
A hand,
Take care of yourself, let your self-love
Expand.
For when you're filled with love, it's easy to
Share,
And make this world a better place,
Showing others you care.

---

33-year-old outdoor enthusiast and passionate writer. Embracing the beauty of nature and capturing through words
Allpoetry.com/Tiffany_Griggs

[ Phoenix Koff ]

# They Ask me Why I Love the Night

when the sun no longer illuminates the sky,
the dark does not blind,
for there is
the light from the stars,
the light from the moon,
illuminating the grounds.

when the sun is gone,
i can finally see,
moonlight illuminating the ground,
seeps into the depths
far beyond imagination
the gentle light follows the breeze,
gliding through the blades of grass,
the forest of an insect just coming out

the light from the orb,
gently glows for us to see
the beauty of the quiet
while everyone else sleeps,
floats down along the wind,
or just through the paths
created by the still air
just specially for the trails of light.

and the stars!
oh the stars,
lights put up by the gods,
scattered among the deep blue,
all so no matter where
in the universe one is,
there will be somewhere to look for light.

all i long for,
all that i live for,
is to one day walk
walk along the path
path of a cemetery
and simply gaze
upon the stones in
the silver light
that flows down
from the beautiful moon.

---

Phoenix is from California, and has used poetry as a creative outlet since middle school. Growing up, they read Edgar Allan Poe and Shel Silverstein. Poe has definitely influenced them more. Allpoetry.com/RavensLenore_Writings

[ The Inner Lens ]

# Threads of False Piety

Beneath the cloak of pious guise,
Men weave the webs, deceit's design,
Akin to the spider in its lies.

With lips reciting text divine,
False piety in hallowed halls,
They stitch the truth with thread malign.

Yet hearts, bound tight by mortal walls,
Sit still, untouched by the Holy Verse,
Perplexed by faith's unanswered calls.

In worship's vice, vice is immersed,
Such a paradox of sacred jest,
In whispered prayers, the cursed converse.

Oh, let the truth rip through this vest,
And bare the soul's unguarded chest!

---

I joined the Navy at 18 and traveled the world. However, upon returning to the United States, I realized that I needed to make some changes to become the person I wanted to be.
Allpoetry.com/The_Inner_Lens

[ Monica Samantha Sanchez ]

# Blue Mark

I used to think I was jaded
At least until I met you
I could lie & say it was fading
But this pain I've gotten used to
Temporary hearts leave lonely scars
& you obnoxiously left your mark
Permanent ink all over this heart
Seeping through my skin
Tinting love forever blue
And I never wanted tattoos

---

Aka ImperFixenBeautySoul/FxNVxN/ Monka626  A mother and nurse, who dive's deep into her heart and writes when it all becomes too heavy. Rough draft written 2022 & Final Draft 'Blue Mark' 2024 Allpoetry.com/FxNVxN

[ Josehf Lloyd Murchison ]
# Melodious Verse

The sweet joy of emotions lived eternal upon the page.
A moment suspended in time by the muses of a melodious heart.
Overflowing with life's winsome passions lived.
Life's woeful sorrows endured.
The touch of the morning sun upon ones face or a lovers kiss upon the lips.
The sweet sent of a flower or the sight of a raptor in flight.
The bittersweet tears of a long lost love.
This made eternal to be relived upon recitation of verse.
This is Poetry.

---

Josehf Lloyd Murchison lives and loves in Ontario Canada where his family and life inspires his writing.
Allpoetry.com/Josehf_Lloyd_Murchison

[ Angel Morgan ]

# Remember Me

Through the blazing fire,
And the driving rain
I had walked.
Over beds of red-hot coals,
and rocky mountain roads
I had traveled.
Within the depths of the sea,
under the scorching sun
I was driven.
I looked everywhere to find your love.
I searched until my mind went crazy.
I looked until my eyes went blind.
I called for you until my voice went mute.
I listened for you until I went deaf.
I dreamed of you until my dreams turned into nightmares.
Even when death itself came for me, you did not remember me.

---

Angel Morgan comes from Mississippi. Writing helps release my inner struggles. I also enjoying video gaming in my spare time. Allpoetry.com/Angel_C_Morgan

[ Charles Gradante ]

# cowboy games

i remember europe
we toasted times gone by
counted the stars
on a beach in sicily
and a gondola in venice

we flew high
with cirque du soleil
swallowed european skies
danced the passion of paris
laughed and cried
then the dawn came

as sunday bells rang
in london
she sang out of tune
oh how i loved her voice
that way

ambrosia perfume
and neon signs
whispered our song

we gave a sigh
to our times gone by

of gentle people
and vintage wines

the days i knew
ended with you

i would never be the same

with a throat of cotton
i rode away
into the sunset

to be forgotten

you may have seen me
i was a cowboy then
playing cowboy games

———————————

Charles Gradante an engineer by education a poet and abstract painter by passion. In expressing the human condition, the arts begin where mere words leave off ...
Allpoetry.com/Charles_Gradante

[ Kathryn Kass ]

# What's In A Name?

Purnima Is a God-given name
signifying wholeness and
the fullness of perfection.

My guru handed it to me on a card,
spelled phonetically.

P-o-o-r-n-i-m-a.

With a sharp breath
I took in only the first four letters,
and perceived all that was lacking in me.

I knew I was poor by any measure.
Did I need to wear my insufficiency
on a name tag, obvious
as a pair of scuffed shoes?

God is not cruel.

However the name is spelled,
the meaning is always the same—
Full Moon.

I reflected on my name,
while bathing in the effulgent light
of cloudless full moon nights.

Like a perfect pearl
that stills the mind
it christened me
with a natural shine
and the luster of tranquility.

But every month
as the light of the moon waned
my thoughts grew darker.
The satisfied sense of repletion abated.
Memories of loss left in the shadows
took form, clearly delineated.

I would remind myself
that the moon is always round and full
while waxing and waning in rhythm with life.
The light is hidden for just one night.

As the moon moved through its phases
from crescent to full and back again
I learned how to welcome the shadows
the way day surrenders to night, slowly,
with sweeping sunsets and creeping twilight.

I would dance with my shadows,
sometimes partnering with madness,
then drop for just one night
into an utterly effacing blackness
to nestle in the empty space between stars,
free from any notion of perfection or imperfection.

I embraced the darkness again and again.
Each time, the light of the crescent moon
would follow, illuminating a path to wholeness
that never privileged light over darkness.

---

My love of meditation, hypnosis, and shamanic journeying is reflected in my work and poetry. I live near the ocean in sunny, southern California, inspired each day by the beauty of nature. Allpoetry.com/Kathryn_Kass

[ Christina M. Cuevas ]
# With God, You Can Overcome Anything

Heaven is such a beautiful place that everyone strives to get into after this life. This is my future home but until than I live each day for you Lord. It is hard in life, we go through many obstacles, but with faith we can overcome it, and then we're blessed in this life for all the hardships we've gone through. So many people have gone through so many things this year and last. But with your beautiful grace, Jesus, I surpass each task daily. I daily walk with you in my heart and in my life. I need you Lord daily and I say a little prayer for the world tonight that's in desperate need for you. Everything seems to be so far from you Lord, with everyone busy - life and things it tends to blind side us all. I hope with a little faith and hope it will be known and told to all. Keep sharing your faith and love to all and always lean on God almighty and his love and you'll get through it. I promise because he is there with you forever. God's love can overcome anything this life may throw at you – so keep going and look up, Heaven is waiting for you always.

---

Estrella - Christina Marie Cuevas, a Texas-born writer, graduated from Everest University with a Bachelor Degree of the Paralegal field.
Allpoetry.com/Lovegurl

[ Maxwell Sebastian Burchett ]

# No Stopping Now

No stopping now.
We will make it somehow.
My only one,
I will take you there.
No stopping now.
No need to worry,
You will be OK.
Love will find a way.
No stopping now.

No matter where,
No matter how far,
Got to be blue skies,
Reaching new highs.
Just hold on,
Hold on to me.
You are never alone.
A new world will be,
What a wonderful world
It will be,
For you and me.
It is our time,
Our day.
We will be OK.

No matter what,
No matter when,
The night may be late,
With you I have always been.
Cannot ever cry.
Always know,
Wherever you go,
We will be OK,
Come what may.
You are beautiful to me,
Always will be,
Day and night,
We will be alright.

No stopping now.
Don't stop now.
There is no stopping now.

---

Max Burchett: a writer, singer and songwriter,
A crooner, a teller of tales,
A dream maker, soul shaker and captivator,
Hoping that in verse and prose he prevails.
Allpoetry.com/MaxBurchett

[ Paul Crocker ]
# Love Me Broken

A relationship isn't always perfect.
It doesn't mean it is not worth it.
Accepting certain aspects of someone's life.
Is showing self-sacrifice.
Love me broken.

Forget the ideal dream.
Let reality break the beam.
Discover hidden beauty in the simple and plain.
Allow the tools of your heart to revive your brain.
Love me broken.

I was whole on a past day.
Now such times have gone away.
I know I can not reclaim the past.
But my spirit remains free to the last.
Love me broken.

---

I am a poet from Bristol, UK. I started writing poems in 2001. I enjoy both reading and writing poetry and everything connected with it. Allpoetry.com/PoeticXscape

[ ALIA Cook ]

# The War Within

A piece of myself is missing.
Rejection and loss, a grief so deep.
My laugh  conceals my despair.
Weighted down by this burden.
Joy is stolen , replaced with darkness.

I gaze at my reflection in the mirror.
This person is a mystery to me.
A voice inside whispers ,you're not enough.
Fear of abandonment is my faithful friend.
Fighting this war within my mind.

Trapped in a cycle, I try to escape.
Remorse and heartache linger.
It stings like a thousand knives.
Someday the pieces will mend.
Even in darkness there is hope.

---

I am a Vegan who lives in the Country. I enjoy foraging, card making , song writing, movies, cooking and music.
Allpoetry.com/Tiedyegirl1976

[ Jim Beitman ]
## we have to let go

we have to let go
peacefully with dignity
cross the rainbow bridge

---

I am an artist living in Noblesville Indiana. Writing is a great media that helps distill my feelings, thoughts, and experiences. It is always a great thrill to be included in an Allpoetry anthology! Allpoetry.com/Beitmanjim

[ James Warren ]

# Untitled 1

When I close my eyes at night
the stars know I dream love true
underneath that moonlit sky
a deeper shade of blue
when the sun rises up
and the day starts anew
a small tear drops from my eye
for I first do not see you.

———————

I am from North Alabama, I enjoy sharing my feelings through writing because sometimes It is hard to speak them. Allpoetry.com/Cosmic_crow

[ Raul Alvarez Viramontes ]
# Solitude

Walk a mile in my shoes

feel the desolation

see the solitude

feel the color of my pain

See the crimson

heart

Share my solitude

explore the vast

emptiness

There I lay

as the world

swirls around me

Fingers through my hair

I rub my shoulder

Walk a mile in my shoes

feel the solitude

---

Born in Long Beach California I've been writing for 62 years. Back when there were mostly farms and the rivers were wild.

Allpoetry.com/Raulviramontes

[ Sophia Kliatchko ]

# Mosaic Heart

Shatter me to pieces....
into delicate shards of glass
I'll only become more beautiful
For in the artist's hands....

Colorful broken fragments
Turn into mosaic art
And indeed, that's my resolve
As I glue back my heart

———————————

A blossoming young poet from the Central Valley, California, Sophia often strives to impart life lessons to her readers by creating metaphors through her muse, Mother Nature. Allpoetry.com/SuperWisdomchild

[ Charles Bateman ]
# The cure

Resentments and grudges are poisonous and deadly
These are the roads of the devil, the path's where
he led me.

They make the heart hard, for evil they groom you
Like anger with hatred, they will all but consume
you.

These nabob's, these demons, influential and daunting,
When you are hooked, it's a shame and exhausting.

This is my attempt to help and to warn you, do away
with all malice and walk in some good shoes.

Pray for a change have some grace and compassion
Now you've heard the cure , put it to action.

_____

I began writing memoirs and poems in my early twenties, I became a published writer two or more years ago. Allpoetry.com/the_budding_warrior

[ Jason E Keeton ]

# An inquiry worth everything

Looking down, would you smile or cry
Think of shame or forgive from a broken sky
You were not alone

Did you feel it take everything away,
as euphoric poison filled inside your tainted veins
You were not alone

You were gone and far away the light
now it seems so long, till we meet where you belong.

Don't you see that I am all to blame,
for the tears that trail your mother's face
You are not alone

Would you open your arms and welcome me
For the sea of guilt, I sank so deep
You are not alone

They say that time heals all wounds,
that's just a lie.
I will have to fight for my life.

---

Jason E Keeton is from Staten Island, NY. With the ambitions of being a musician, Jason E Keeton put his dreams of music on hold and joined the United States Navy where he turns his music into poetry. Allpoetry.com/Jason_E._Keeton

[ Sam Y. Berry ]
# A light in the dark

Once, it boiled.
It just had to come out and it did.
It came out violently, yet slowly.
I did not see it coming.
I felt it through my brain like a spin, a whirl, a storm, a tempest.
Once, it was here.
Buried in me but who could help me?
Then, there was nothing I could feel.
I was empty.
You helped me through it.
Some did not believe me but you were there.
I know it was not easy.
I know I made you cry.
I know you cried with me.
Eventhough we never do this.
I found out it will never be the same as it was before all this.
Is it what being an adult feels like?
No one had told me it was brutal.
As I always say, I was born nervous.
That's how I know you understand, because you and me are the same.
You gave me life and then, you gave me light.

───────────────

My pen name is Sam Y. Berry. Sam was the name of my father's German Shepherd when I was born. Y is the first letter of my late grand-father and Berry is short for my actual last name. I'm 28, french. Allpoetry.com/Sam_Y._Berry

[ Nancy Carol Warrender ]

# The Best December Ever

*A duet with my pet ladybug*

Weather your winter is warm or cold
there will be a holiday song

I hope it's not too long

While flying through the aisles of the grocery store
for me it's not just a weekly chore
I like the pears, roast beef, and brownies
today there's some out-of-townies
there is even food for a dog
but what is this stuff called eggnog?

I've tasted the fancy fruitcakes
reindeer shaped chocolates in foil
end the end of an aisle!
I must make a quick stop, for a cardboard stand of old bearded
man shaped lollipop?
I must admit the idea is mighty clever
Wishing you the Best December Ever!

I am off to the beach, flying over the sand
I sure hope your December holiday is grand!
The trees have grown lights!
They warm my nights.

I'm careful 'round the candles
watching every ember
and wishing you the very best December.

the radio says it is New Years Eve
What does a ladybug do tonite,
Whatever she please
so far it's been the Best December Ever!

---

Born 1964 in Norwich, Connecticut. Bachelor of Science in Business Administration 1986. Currently resides in North Carolina. Allpoetry.com/Nancy_Carol_Warrender

[ Robert J Owens ]
# Each Dawn I Die

My biggest regret
Is not being there for you
And not doing all of the things
That dad's supposed to do

But don't misconstrue
Because each dawn, i die
And in my moments of solitude
I can't help but cry

But life is still good
Full of hidden lessons
And if you cant find forgiveness
Then I've learned my lesson

And if we can't reconcile
I'll understand why
I just needed you to know
That each dawn, I die.

---

Dedicated to Catherine A. Owens. I'm from Los Angeles CA and has always had a love for poetry and song writing and would very much like to write a whole book of poems and create a beautiful and respected body of work . Allpoetry.com/Krownroyal007

[ Elizabeth Brushia ]

# God's Paintbrush

He laid the paintbrush at your hand,
to paint it out for me.
Images of sacrafice
Behold the Trinity.
As the brush continues on..
Deepened, darkened hues,
To each of us free will he gave,
Which color will you choose?
Placed upon your palette
Intensified is red
Illustrating suffrages,
With battles and bloodshed.
Along with all these colors
Lay softened shades of blue,
That represents eternal light
this cross he boar for you.
So choose your colors wisely.
With sacraments and grace.
Painting with his glory,
Ease struggles that we face.
God holds the hand,
To guide the brush..
Your journey spreads his word.
Speaking everlasting life,
That lies upon our lord.

---

I am from Stevensville Mt, emotional thought and with so many dynamics to life I can't process into words for someone to understand the depth of a feeling. Poetry became the only way I understood it  Allpoetry.com/Zilliz81

[ Adelina Morris ]

# The Eyes

The eyes see what they want to see
But its the heart that sees what the eyes don't

---

My name is Adelina Morris. I am from California. I enjoy writing and I love that people can relate to what I write. I try to inspire and give to the paper 100% of my heart.
Allpoetry.com/nicoleray91

[ Nicole Shunk ]

# Broken Path

Devotion
Attachment
Friendship
Windfall of the heart
Twin flames
Soul mates
Star crossed lovers
Embodiments of being in love
When that love ceases to exist
It transforms into
Fragmented
Erratic
Sorrowfulness
Inconsolable grief
Loss of a blue moon partner
Broken assurances
Barren Dreams
Musings
Of old age together
A bench built for two
Now splintered like my heart
I'm sure how to heal
How to find my way
To the comeback trail
My heart keeps

Giving me the slip
With each beat my resilience grows
The pain may never end
Grief will last my entire existence
Healing and growth will continue
As my lifetime will too

---

Nicole Shunk is a southern born who call the north home. Poetry is an art that saved my life. Now I share my writing and hope these words help and inspire others. Allpoetry.com/Shunket23

[ Dr. Monica Discolo ]
# I'm only here because of you

maybe someday you'll see how I
adore you beyond measure, and how
through my eyes you are without flaw
a perfectly decorated canvas, covered in
your favorite things in permanent ink
a picture of beauty you refuse to see

forgetting all you have endured
like it never happened will take work,
each day we will work the scars left behind
until they are barely visible to the outside world
replaced with love and everything spooky
and together we will build a life we can love

---

Dr. Monica Discolo is a published writer, artist, photographer, crafter, and researcher. She is from Boston, Massachusetts but lives in Clearwater, Florida. 'I live the poetry I cannot write.' Allpoetry.com/Dr._Borden's_Axe

[ Marcus Taylor ]

# Mother can you hear me..

How distant you have grown
How close I have followed
How can you still laugh, smile and sing
My tortured angel,
I try to understand this alien communication
But' I'm lost in your eyes
Your eyes are desperate and confused
My eyes are tearful and weak,
Mother can you hear me...

---

Marcus Taylor  born on sheppey
South East Kent, England
My passion is listening and collecting progressive music of the 60s/70s but I enjoy writing poetry mostly in free verse and rhyme
Allpoetry.com/Marcus_taylor

[ Gordon Hoffman ]

# Barbara

Barbara sits in a flooded street
her love's an ocean, she's in too deep
her eyes drip like stream room ceilings
her nose runs with beautiful feelings
but she can't get too far...
when he hits her like an armoured car
she's humpty dumpty as she falls apart
You should know, Barbie, that love is a contact sport

I love you I love you till you die
although you're over there Barbara Ann
He cheated, he cheated and he lied
he wasn't true Barbara Ann
But I am, yes I am and I never had a care
but I care about you Barbara Ann

Barbara Ann, I understand you

She lies on the floor
Can't stand her emotions anymore
she paints her nails with a loveless touch
she sees his face and her fingers blush
She feels him hit her like an armoured car,
decides she needs CPR because she's dying inside
she's crying tears behind her clotted eyes
while he's swinging on her stair

and singing Cruel to Be Kind
she's lost in despair without a care

I love you I love you till you die
although you're over there Barbara Ann
He cheated, he cheated and he lied
he wasn't true Barbara Ann
But I am, yes I am and I never ever stare
but I stare at you, Barbara Ann

Barbara Ann, I understand you

my heart is breaking with beautiful feelings
my eyes are dripping like stream room ceilings
my face is on display, without you, barbie, I'm not ok

your fingers are much too much
they carry the Lubitsch touch
girl I'll be your medicine man
I'll heal your heart Barbara Ann

Barbara Ann, I understand
I'd hate to lose you, Barbara Ann

---

Gordon Hoffman is a writer of honesty, trouble, and whatever nonsense plagues his weary head. He plots his poems through lost weekends and whisky. He thinks too much.
Allpoetry.com/Gordon_Hoffman

[ Manju Kabba ]

# Halt It Now

Unease apparent, a ripple of discussions unfolds,
Maturity for gruesome mutilation, seemingly growing old.

Traditional requirements, a distant, impractical fetch,
The victim's labor a remedy, a daunting, unjust task.

Porwulor, on edge, her friends now scarred,
False prominence claimed, a facade marred.

Now Porwulor's turn, emotions high,
Chalked and cloaked, escorted, oh my!
In the bush, a doctor without mercy or gear,
In this age and time, the ideal must disappear.

Her scream echoes, helpless and in pain,
Faints away, bleeding, a life in vain.
In the bush, her remains interred,
Tradition calls for no alarm, and truth never heard.

A lie boldly told to her grieving father,
A favorite she became, forever to bother.

Let's not believe in this archaic vow,
For the sake of girls in Africa, it must be eradicated now!

───────────────

Manju Kabba is a dedicated educator and passionate researcher with over 15 years of experience in the field of education, primarily in Liberia. Throughout his career, he has collaborated with schools. Allpoetry.com/Manju_Kabba

[ Gregory Bernal ]

## Angel's Kiss

Written with expression, words come to life,
Deep in his thoughts as the poet writes,
Not just words but part of his soul,
Cages open as his heart let's go.

High as a bird soaring under the sun,
Flying through the night till the morning comes,
Freeing of your mind I might express,
Peace of the soul, like an angel's kiss.

Laughter and pain inked on these pages,
Giving you chills as his soul reveals loves many rages,
An allusion, a rhyme the words set to tone,
These sheets penned are his open heart being shown!

---

My name is Greg and I write under the pseudo I am Z Ro. I've been writing since I was 12. A few years ago I started writing again. Writing is truly a way to find peace within yourself thank you. Greg Allpoetry.com/I_am_Z_Ro

[ Laura Gallagher ]

# I miss

I miss her laughter that would echo through the house,
Her cigarette burning as she told another tale,
Sitting crossed legged in her favourite chair,
Perfectly positioned by the window she can pause and stare,
I miss her words of wisdom when all else failed,
Her stroke of optimism and faith would restart your day,
Her soft smile and glistening eyes tell a story of laughter and play,
A strong and brave woman she once was,
Very few got the best of her she rose above every time,
Making sure her doubters would applause,
Her thick skin and sass would always shine,
I miss her olden day qoutes she seemed to have for every ailment,
Her tips and tricks and pure devilment,
My heart will long for her 'til it is my time,
Even in mourning she makes me smile and grin,
With all the ways she was perfectly human,
A life lived, you deserve this peace and rest.

───────────────

Hello, I am Laura, I am from the west of Ireland. Poetry for me is a great way to clarify feelings and put meaning to them. Tones to my poems are journeys we take and overall message of love and light Allpoetry.com/Laura_Gallagher

[ Nancy Carol Warrender ]
# Dragon Fruit Punch

Under the sun, under the moon
Under the sun, under the moon

I'm sitting in the sun but you can't see me
It's warm, relaxing, uplifting
orange, is my favorite color - today
the light bounces off the nearby water
I'm drinking dragon fruit punch

A garden full of greens and reds
my pet turtle and my pet frog
remembering the sun is a star
the center of our solar system

maybe you can't see us here
maybe you can't find us
even underneath the sun

I can hear laughter from the swimming pool
Do I dare walk over there wearing a rose lace bikini?
I guess you really did make a big splash

maybe you can find me

we're under the sun, under the moon
under the sun, under the moon
under the sun, under the moon

(whispered)
Under the sun, Under the moon

---

Amateur songwriter in North Carolina.  US Copyright 2013.
Born 1964 in Norwich, Connecticut.  Bachelor of Science Business
Administration 1986. Allpoetry.com/Nancy_Carol_Warrender

[ Dr. Nafees Alam ]

# Strong, Intelligent Man's Pledge

*A Shakespearean Sonnet*

Half my education, you have not earned,
All my youth, I built mind, body, soul, wealth.
Half my transformation, your love I yearned,
All your truth, encompassing none my health.
You rode the carousel, the phase of ho,
My growth so lonesome, no shoulder for tears.
You hit the wall, crass cliches apropo,
My oath: focused success, no love for years.
But half of mine is all for you, my queen,
Smell all the roses and take your sweet time.
For all of mine has been for you, my queen,
Awaiting patient for your day past prime.
My commitment to you need not a hedge,
For this is strong, intelligent man's pledge.

---

Dr. Nafees Alam is a professor of social work at Boise State University. After a long career in the social sciences, he is looking to expand his horizons into the world of literary art. Allpoetry.com/Nafees_Alam

Printed in Great Britain
by Amazon